KING ME

How To Beat Abuse and Become a Success

T-Penn,
I appreciate the
support. I hope you enjoy
the Reading

Published by:
Fortune Publishing Group
E-mail: info@fortunepublishinggroup.com
www.FortunePublishingGroup.com

Phone: (443) 256-3400

Printed in the United States of America

Cover Layout: Max Fortune

DEDICATION

To my family, Kim, Courtney, Torie, Dorien & Nicholas, words cannot explain how much I cherish you. Thank you for being there through everything. Your happiness is my bliss. You are my inspiration 100% of the time.

To Auntie, heaven received its missing angel. You came into my life for a reason and made an impact immediately. You helped me through my moments of Alchemy. I love you, and you will always live in my heart.

To my mother, I love you, and I always will. You understanding the importance of this project is a testament to us continuing to build our love for each other and God.

Contents

INTRODUCTION

Many decades have passed since my ancestors were taken from the Continent of Africa and tortured while they built the infrastructure of this country. A still untold number of Africans were violently taken from their lands and placed in bondage all over the globe. Those who landed in the United States were turned into slaves and used to cultivate sugar cane, cotton and other crops, while their slave masters were able to amass great wealth resulting from the work they performed. America has greatly benefited from having free labor for centuries as a result of the slave trade. Many slaves were banned from benefiting from the work of their own hands, while simultaneously being prohibited from entering the same buildings and using the bridges and structures they built. Slavery is an evil and horrible blood stain in the garments of America. I do not celebrate or support the enslavement of my people for the betterment of other ethnic groups. I do, however, recommend and strongly suggest that my people start using the skills we acquired during slavery to build our own dreams and businesses. Those acquired project management, engineering, carpentry, and construction skills were valuable to my ancestors. Those skills, along with a working knowledge of banking and business development, is crucial to the growth of our communities.

Although slavery is "technically" abolished in America, there are still systematic methods of enslavement in place that prove to be worse than the physical enslavement we faced during the Colonial period of America's history.

Every Black man who has suffered traumatically in life must be able to draw connections and find parallels between the struggles he faces and the useful set of skills that can be acquired to push him into greater success. Young Black men raised in the bowels of America have endured hard times that can push them into incredible potential and accomplishments. Countless young men raised in urban and rural settings didn't attend college because their parents couldn't afford to send them. Others had to get a job to help support their families. Perhaps they've even found themselves caught up in the judicial system because of unfair targeting by police or policies designed to negatively impact their futures. So, to survive, they turn to activities like selling drugs or protecting the local drug dealer. Noticed, but not deeply understood, these young men develop hands-on skills that are stronger than any information books, academic tests, or a collegiate experience could provide.

Take into consideration an 18-year-old young man who begins selling drugs to survive an expensive and demanding existence in New York City. He must first generate startup money to cover the initial cost of buying the drugs to sell. Once the initial cost is met, he needs to create a business plan that includes target markets, pricing for his product, a packaging and logistics strategy, securing protection to ensure his product isn't stolen, and lastly, a profit/loss (P/L) model that confirms the growth of his business. After establishing a good base for his business, he may find it necessary to grow by merging with other business owners who look like him. This kind of collaboration provides another strong skill set that teaches negotiation, organizational restructuring, and streamlining of business tactics. Multiple soft skills are even more essential to acquire in this scenario, such as people management, emotional intelligence, and ensuring customer satisfaction. All of these skills are desirable in big corporations because they increase the bottom line. I know most Americans will find it very difficult to view a drug dealer as a businessman because the act is unlawful and adverse to the way we view people who engage in such nefarious deeds. But he is a businessman in every sense of the word. The chances of a 20-year-old drug dealer being better educated than a 20-year-old business college student is more likely than America would like to believe, but if you consider the value of hands-on experience gleaned by the man in the street, you might agree that it's possible. Remove drugs from the business model and replace them with cars or real estate, and you have a model easily sanctioned and replicated by Corporate America. I am not advocating for young Black men to sell drugs, but I am suggesting they be intentional about creating a better life for themselves and their communities with those skills. And I'm also suggesting they open their minds to reframing the way they view the skills they've developed. We must be able to glean best practices from past successful community models like Tulsa, Oklahoma's community known as Black Wall Street. We must develop and leverage all the skills needed to create successful and thriving communities in every city across America.

PURPOSE

The American Black male is endangered, and therefore, the Black family in America is also compromised. With access to the now commonplace invention of the computer and a limited ability to leverage the internet, one can research as much official U.S. Census data as they please. And with that data, one might be forced to conclude that the African-American race is in trouble. The Black family is on pace to be more irrelevant than at any other time in history if we do not pay attention to the numbers.

In 2018, the U.S. Census estimated that 323 million Americans are living in the United States. Of out the entire population, 42.5 million (13%) are considered Black. Based on the number of Blacks in the U.S., 19.9 million (6%) are males. And of the 19.9 Black males, approximately 7.7 million (2%) are under 25-years-of age. To clarify, as of 2018, young Black males under the age of 25 years, constitute only 2% of the entire U.S. population and are expected to contribute to the Black community's growth.

In comparison, whites make up 196 million (61%) of the U.S. population. Based on that number, approximately 96 million (30%) are males. And of the 96 million white males, approximately 27 million (8%) are under 25-years-of age. That is 8% of the American population that are young white males alone which is four times greater than African American males. What that means is, by sheer numbers, Black males must compete for jobs, education, business loans, and everything else in life against a population in which he only constitutes 2%.

The Black male must be strong, smart, and understands how to hustle; so he can work through such an imbalance. However, other considerations, such as the lack of educational achievement, their increasing presence in the prison population, and the rate at which Black males are being murdered must also be factored into these numbers.

Based on the same data set, out of the 7.7 million Black males, only 450,000 (6%) attain a bachelor's degree or higher, compared to other ethnic groups.

If you rewind the data for just ten years, there were 301 million people and 37 (12.2%) million African Americans. The American population continues to increase. In America, someone is being born approximately every eight seconds, according to the latest US Census data estimates. And if those being born happen to be Black and Male, they will very likely face impossible odds to survive into early adulthood--and by the time they reach the age of maturity, many of them have experienced many forms of trauma—including, and especially, racial trauma. I believe that Black American men experience traumatizing events on a more consistent basis than their counterparts.

I have written this book because I felt it was important to share horrific experiences from my past with my brothers so I can demonstrate how I have used these experiences to fuel my success. Very often, the notion of turning your negative experiences into positive ones is considered trite and somewhat cliché. However, the ability, desire, and persistence needed to turn negatives into positives is extremely difficult to acquire. It is far easier to engage in endless banter and creative excuse-making sessions rather than to live one's life doing the work. Thus, the more significant achievement is to transition from a life of sorrow and long-suffering into a life of success and prosperity.

Let's get this straight right now; this book is not just another "woe-is-me-story-of-my-life" kind of story. I'll save that for another writer. Although this book is a sincere accounting of my life's events, the telling is from the perspective of one Black man to another about how we can turn our horrific experiences into strength-building opportunities. This book will focus on how it is inevitable and necessary for us to rise from the flames of society to fly further than we have before. By revisiting my traumatic life experiences, I've discovered the skills and talents I developed as a result of them. I've been able to gain an understanding of what one must do when turning undesirable metals into opulent materials that are fit for a king. Here, I will share what I have learned with you. Enjoy the rest of the book.

~

PART-ONE

Alchemy

For hundreds of years, alchemy has been a science that remains a mystery to man. Always thought to be the foundation of what we now identify as chemistry, alchemy is the supposed transformation of matter. Alchemy is also defined as the attempted conversion of base metals into gold. For as long as the practice of alchemy has existed, the concept has been met with fear, suspicion, and dark perception. Because it is often considered black magic, sorcery, or witchcraft, the mention of the word "alchemy" creates disbelief and adverse judgment.

There is a more subtle and universal definition of alchemy as the transformation, combination, or creation of any one thing into something else. Before a family sits down to have dinner, the parents combine meats, grains, vegetables, and spices to create a meal, and if done correctly, it is devoured by the recipients of this alchemic practice. But wait, dinner isn't scary! Having a delicious meal with family as you engage in mediocre banter about that day's experiences is hardly considered black magic. In fact, it feels more like the catalyst for love. We often derive great pleasure from taking one thing and transforming it into something different and unique.

The American Black male is a master of alchemy based on the second definition. The alchemy of the Black male is both literal and figurative. For centuries, he has shown the world his ability to transform meager rations of food, materials, and knowledge into a foundation that explodes into wealth. It is not uncommon for an

African American male to grow up in the slums of New York City, Chicago, Los Angeles, Miami, Atlanta, or Dallas and build massive amounts of wealth in his lifetime. Starting with literally nothing, countless African American businessmen such as Samuel Wilcox, Magic Johnson, and Jay Z have amassed great wealth as a result of their sheer efforts and their will to succeed. But the mentality was set even during slavery.

According to website Tech. Co, Robert Gordon was born a slave and eventually purchased his freedom in 1846. In 1847, he invested $15,000 in a Cincinnati coal yard and employed bookkeepers and laborers. White coal dealers in Cincinnati attempted to price Gordon out of the market by selling their coal below market rates. Gordon employed mulattoes to purchase the cheaper coal, eventually selling the supply at a high price after the white coal dealers had little left in their reserves (Ronald Barba, 2015).

Tech.co also establishes John H. Johnson as a renowned businessman and publisher. He is the founder of Johnson Publishing Company, which publishes both *Ebony* and *Jet* magazines. *The Negro Digest*, the predecessor to Johnson's *Ebony*, was his attempt to create a publication for the black community that mimicked the style of the *Reader's Digest*. To fund that initial venture, Johnson used a $500 loan he borrowed against his mother's furniture. In 1982, Johnson became the first African-American to appear on the Forbes 400 list. Currently, the Johnson Publishing Company employs more than 2,600 people and has sales of nearly $400 million (John H. Johnson, 2015).

I believe this is all alchemy because of how they acquired wealth. The Black man has had no slaves working tirelessly to bring him great wealth. He almost seems like a magician--using grand showmanship to turn a plastic dove into the real breathing animal that takes flight.

That's why alchemy is synonymous with the African American male's history. The American society has a shamefully long and gruesome history of stacking the deck against Blacks, with particular attention to Black men. And, like magicians, they consistently and out of nowhere, overcome the odds and succeed.

As an example, "the blues" is a genre of music that was created by Black Southern plantation slaves of the 19th century who sang songs of sorrow as they worked in the fields. Despite the environment, the slaves combined their pain and innate musical talent to grow the genre into an enduring piece of Americana. This genre produced such stars as B.B. King, Muddy Waters, Jimi Hendrix, and Eric Clapton. Jazz, another musical genre, is a direct descendant of blues. Both are the result of slaves taking advantage of their talents and conditions and creating something different, new, and profitable-- that is alchemy.

~

The Phoenix

The Phoenix is a bird from <u>Greek mythology that is said to be reborn</u> from the <u>ashes</u> of its predecessor. Black men in America are not magical birds, but they do take on the characteristics of the fairy tale creature. They are consistently burned by abuse and mistreatment from other ethnicities. However, lifetime after lifetime, they pick themselves up and move forward. The concept of living like a Phoenix is an analogy that Black men have always embodied, especially in America.

The idea of Black men resembling the Phoenix is not a new way of thinking. This concept dates to ancient Egyptian civilization. Horus, for instance, is the ruler of the gods and is represented by a falcon. He was also known as the patron saint of the existing pharaoh. The pharoah was referred to as the "Living Horus." Horus was the son of Ra, the sun god. Whenever a pharaoh dies, his body was believed to be united with the sun while a new Horus ruled on earth. Essentially, Horus, the god, was reborn from the ashes of the previous pharaoh, like a Phoenix. No matter the condition, Black men must always get back up, dust the ashes off and fly further than they did before. So, hustle, grind, get it in, young fella…. get it in!

My Story

My childhood memories of Pelham, Georgia are somewhat typical of any young Black boy growing up when I did. I see images of myself in my mind's eye—running around in the pecan groves playing with my brother while my mother collected thousands of hard-shelled nuts into buckets. My brother and I would have to go to work with my mom because there was no money for daycare, and the family members who could possibly babysit were also in the dew-covered fields scraping pecans from the carpet of the earth.

Pelham is a sleepy little rural town that feels like it could be the scene from a movie about it being discovered by some city slicker looking for a place to hide out from his real life. When you live in a town that has a population of around 3,500 people, everyone knows each other and are probably related, and this is the case for Pelham.

The roads were narrow and run down because the local government didn't have enough money to build a robust infrastructure. Grass, shrubs, and weeds line either side of the street. Old, rusted industrial and farm equipment sit aging in overgrown fields between the bungalow-style homes perched on concrete cinder blocks.

Money, like hope, was scarce. My grandparents had twelve children, so our family was very large. My grandfather and one of my aunts died before I was five, leaving my grandmother to support a family of eleven on her own. Jobs are always hard to come by in small, rural towns. There was a local peanut factory that harvested and processed the peanuts grown by nearby farmers, and

Those peanut mills with rusted silos occupied a permanent place near the center of town. My grandmother worked at the same peanut factory for as long as I can remember. One of my fondest memories I have is of my grandmother bringing peanuts home for the kids to enjoy. Whether they were boiled or roasted in the oven and salted, the peanuts were always a treat. This would be my grandmother's source of income for many years. My grandmother was the anchor of our family, and I have always respected her strength and ability to set direction for an entire family.

I have vague memories of my grandfather cooking pork skins in the backyard in a huge, black metal cauldron. I always thought of pictures I found in books of witches cooking children whenever he lit the fire and began his weekly ritual.

Growing up, most of my very large family thought I was weird because I asked questions; I was naturally curious. Consequently, I would often break things due to my curiosity and wanting to understand how they worked. In a large humble family like mine, grown-ups didn't appreciate children who tamper with things they worked hard to buy. Even at the age of 4, I felt alienated and neglected.

The Goody's hair comb factory was in Pelham, too, but those jobs remained with those who were lucky enough to be hired—there was hardly ever any job openings for this reason. My mother was fortunate to land a position on the Goody's assembly line. With the meager wages from the factory, she managed to move into a house of her own with me and my older brother Tommy.

As I continued to grow, I became even more inquisitive and wanted to learn everything I possibly could, so college became a goal for me fairly early. But college graduation isn't an aspiration that was shared by my mother's family. Neither my mother nor any of her siblings even graduated high school.

My parents were never married. I was the product of a high school fling, so I never knew much about my father. However, I later learned that my father's family was very educated and lived all across America. I imagine that was due to the experiences their education afforded them. Their professions varied greatly—there were corporate managers, clergymen, and IT professionals among them. Even though education was something I had in common with my father's family, I had no relationship with any of them. I vaguely remember going to visit my grandmother once or twice, and that is the only memory I have of my father's family, so most of my childhood memories involve my mother's family. And although they are memories of miseducation and dysfunction, there are a few sprinkles of joy here and there.

When I was seven my mother married a local preacher and we moved to Thomasville, Georgia. Thomasville's history is stained with all of the unimaginable atrocities that took place on Southern plantations in the United States. Thomasville is five times as large as Pelham, but it was still a typical small, Southern town; although it had a population of about 20,000, it seemed like we'd moved to the big city.

There are two perspectives one could use when viewing Thomasville, Georgia. One viewpoint is that it had lots of what America refers to as "southern charm and beauty" because many of its large plantations were converted into hotels and private clubs and massive oak tree-lined sidewalks. Charming little Thomasville can be perceived as happy, slow-paced, and picturesque. However, the history of slavery and the awful experiences those enslaved people must have endured in a place that is, still today, saturated with "old money" and monuments to those very plantation owners somewhat ruins this view for any person of African descent.

Thomasville's unemployment rate is high--which translates into neighborhoods of row houses sitting on concrete blocks that line slender streets. These houses are also remnants of that era because these streets are where the former slaves were made to live and grow their families. These are the unspoken, unfair things that one notices about life growing up in the South, but no language can adequately convey that feeling when you're young. Now that I'm grown, I can see it clearly and admit that, in spite of those things, there are parts of Thomasville that are breathtakingly beautiful.

For instance, the "Big Oak" is a 308-year-old oak tree that towers over the corner of Monroe and Crawford streets. While many white Americans consider such a natural beauty a historic jewel, Black Americans may view it through the lens of lynchings that undoubtedly took place there. That same thing of beauty can also serve as an awful memory of social injustices that still plague us today.

Thomasville's demographics are unique because the city is almost even in the number of Black and white citizens. Approximately 43% of the city is called home by Blacks, and around 55% of its population is White. That is an unusual demographic for any city, and it's been that way for decades. Therefore, there is palpable racial tension that is undeniable.

There is one thing for sure: football is big in Thomasville, very big! Countless state championships and even more professional football players are launched into NFL fame from our two high schools. My move to this charming, picturesque, racially tense city was the epitome of a bitter and sweet experience.

Stacked Against Me

Even before I was born, life built a fortress around success to prevent my entry. I grew up in an impoverished, neglectful, and abusive home environment. My entire community seemed to reflect what I saw at home. Everything appeared to be a maze of red clay infrastructures connected to the remnants of a few unmaintained asphalt roads that were neglected by the local government long ago. Even the stores along the short, uninspiring streets seemed cold, empty and neglected. The first five years of my life I seemed to have lived in black and white--without energy, and with very little. Therefore, a sense of helplessness immediately overcomes me when I reflect on my childhood.

As I mentioned, I never had a relationship with my father. I remember meeting him when I was around the age of five. There wasn't much of an explanation about why my father wasn't in my life from any of the adults in my family. But although I was living in an impoverished and abusive environment without the guidance of a father, for as early as I can remember, I dreamed about overcoming these obstacles and making a good life for myself. Nobody told me that the journey would be so long and tough, but thankfully, I had the desire and the proper spirit that would allow me to achieve.

Not Your Soccer Mom

My mother terrorized me when I was growing up. She was always so angry and confrontational. I could never put my finger on what I did that made her not love me, but I believed it must have been *something*! So, I worked harder to make good grades. I was always a fairly smart child, and nothing would have meant more to me than to have my mother admire that about me and compliment me for my cleverness. Instead, I received constant anger or absolute neglect. Her behavior confused me because everywhere else, I was recognized and admired for being smart, but she made me feel like being smart was nothing special. She made me feel like I was nothing special. But there was something inside me that let me know I was both smart and special!

I remember being so proud of myself when I first learned the term "yesteryear" from my 3rd-grade teacher. I was so excited to share my new word with my mom. This was before I realized that she was never going to be impressed by what I knew. At that moment, though, I felt smart--genius even! I imagined myself finally getting the attention and love I wanted from her. I could barely hold my excitement.

But my mother was not home when I got there, so, unfortunately, my excitement would have to wait two hours. I'm not sure why I was surprised because my mother was never there when we got back from school. We were "latch key kids"--which meant when we came home from school, we were alone until our parents or other caregivers arrived; usually, this was within a couple of hours.

I was so excited that I checked the window every 15 minutes or so, hoping she would be early. But it would be closer to three hours before my mother and my stepfather would come home. By now, it was close to 6 pm, so my brother and I were miserable and hungry. I was aware that my mother was probably tired from her long day, but I still wanted to share with her what I learned that day. I just enjoyed learning so much as a child that I wanted to share my findings with everyone-- but mainly, my mother.

She walked in the door with her usual demeanor, pre-occupied and angry, and I instantly became nervous and fidgety. I was afraid she would yell at me for rushing her as soon as she arrived home. So, while the excitement was killing me, fear won that particular battle, and my excitement subsided.

So, my brother and I went out to play football for a while. But my mind was still fixed on talking with my mother. I didn't share it with my brother because I didn't feel the need to impress him. We were the best of friends, and I already had his love. But, more than anything in the world, I wanted my mother to be proud of me. I really wanted her love and acceptance.

Tommy and I finally went in and had dinner, which usually consisted of something quick, greasy, and fatty. Afterward, I finally mustered up enough courage to begin the conversation. I thought it best to use the term in a sentence, so I said, "Momma, guess what?! I was seven yester-year."

I placed a huge confident smile on my face that showed I knew what I was saying, and I was damn proud of it! There was an uncomfortable pause that filled the room and replaced my palpable joy with a deafening silence that immediately caused me to revert to nervousness and shame. After what felt like forever, my mother and step-father burst into laughter. I thought to myself, Wait....what? I didn't mean for that to be funny. Although yesteryear isn't standard language, it can be used without confusing the person with whom you're communicating. I was confused. Why were they laughing? That wasn't what I wanted at all.

My mother finally responded and said, "that's not a word, boy," as she continued to chuckle dismissively.

Immediately, the rebellious side of me jumped to my defense. I responded, "yes, but it is a 'term.' People use it when they talk about last year," I further argued my point.

My mother's face became very serious, and I knew from that look I was in trouble. My mother had a very quick temper and was intolerant of children talking back to any grown-up regardless of the circumstance.

She repeated herself this time with more force and authority than before, "Corey, go somewhere making stuff up."

"But it *is* a term!" I quickly and sharply responded without once considering the consequences--or my safety, for that matter. I could tell my last statement got under my mother's skin. She began yelling with anger and contempt. Her words became a blur to me at this point because I was crushed and saddened that my expression of intelligence didn't bring me the response I desired. Instead, it brought me ridicule and anger. I was baffled, upset, and angry at this point. Why is it that I could never get her approval?

I defiantly blurted out, "you don't know, my teacher taught it to me earlier. Why can't you believe me?"

Within a second of my outburst, I felt excruciating pain explode from the left side of my face. It felt like a thousand killer bees had landed on it and stung me all at once. My mother put all her might into slapping me for responding to her in such a forceful manner. She was infuriated that I had voiced my opinion, and she was determined to teach me not to express my feelings even if I was correct.

In retrospect, this moment reminds me of a slave master's attempt to break the ones that dared to speak out. I felt as if I was a slave. I wasn't allowed to be smart. I wasn't allowed to speak out about what mattered to me most. My mother was the slave master that needed control, power, and respect--even if it meant beating me into submission.

Similar scenarios continued throughout the years. In another incident, I was around the same age, and my mother, brother, and I were visiting my stepfather's relatives. My mother and Tonya, my stepfather's sister, were sitting in the den watching television while my brother and I sat on the floor beside my mother. That was always our position, on the floor beside her feet. (To this day, I hate for my kids to be on the floor.)

Tommy, my brother, and I were quietly talking, entertaining ourselves because the program didn't keep our attention. My mother said to us, "shut up that fuss." She never liked for kids to make a lot of noise. We did just as she asked for about three minutes, but the program was so boring to us that we started up a conversation again.

I assume she was finally fed up because she slapped me on the face hard enough to cause an eye bleed. I don't remember the look on Aunt Tonya's face, and I don't recall my brother's response, but I do know I screamed uncontrollably in terror and pain. But my outcry was met with more punishment. I tried to control my crying to avoid another assault, so I covered my mouth as blood dripped down my hand onto the floor.

I heard Aunt Tonya say, "Phyllis, you ain't gotta hit them kids like you do, nah." At that moment, I thought I had a protector. I was temporarily saved from the brutal master I serve.

My mother boldly responded, "these are my kids, you don't tell me how to raise them. Worry about your own stuff."

That's when I discovered even the adults around us could not protect me. I was afraid and confused. I wanted to know why she hated me so much.

The beatings continued throughout adolescence, until one pivotal point that would help me escape the spiritual, mental, and physical abuse of my mother. Now, although I was an intelligent kid, I got bored very easily, so I always found myself in trouble while trying to keep myself occupied. However, I would never do anything major; my offenses were small, like teasing my younger brother. Teasing my younger brother Chuck was the beginning of my great escape because it would trigger events that would ultimately push me out of my mother's home.

One day, I was teasing him as I usually did. I was thirteen, and Chuck, was five at the time. We were in the small, congested living room. My mother and stepfather occupied the only couch in the room, while my brothers and I sat and wrestled lightly, as boys do. My sons play this way all the time as a way to bond. And, as older brothers sometimes will, I held my younger brother's arms so he couldn't move. At this point, my younger brother usually cries when he's fed up with not being able to move. As expected, he started crying.

My mother immediately became angry and slapped the back of my head and said, "stop hurting that boy."

I responded, "I didn't hurt him; he's just a cry baby."

Well, something about that statement didn't sit with my mother, because she began hitting me in the back. At this age, I was bigger than my mother, so her hands didn't hurt anymore. She had increased my tolerance for pain by beating me so much. But I wasn't happy with being punished because of such an innocent misunderstanding.

Without thinking, I became rebellious. I jumped up and screamed, "Don't hit me no more." I looked at my brother as if I was asking to be rescued. Shock and fear filled his eyes in response as if to say to me, "What are you doing? You have gone mad, man!. She is going to *kill* you."

I couldn't control my response to the beating; I was fed up with being a punching bag. At that point, I was back to feeling like the rebellious slave who so badly wanted to be removed from the dangerous environment before it sent me to an early grave. I wanted freedom, even if it meant dying for it. My home environment was as toxic as any plantation, in many ways. Spiritually, physically, and mentally, I was treated like a captured servant, and so I was dead set on escaping.

"Who do you think you are talking to?" my mother screamed uncontrollably. "Go back to that room and wait for me," she continued.

I stormed out of the room--actually happy to leave the situation, but in complete disbelieve. I felt as if I had stood up to the slave master. Instead of being frightened I was calm and at peace like a brick had been lifted from my chest, and I was finally breathing. I had been suffocated by neglect and abuse since birth, and being in an unsafe environment was increasing the speed at which I would die. Many scenarios ran through my head as I waited for what would come next from my mother.

I heard footsteps becoming louder as I waited behind the paper-thin door. I was filled with fear when I heard her angrily say, "Imma beat the life out of him."

She burst through the door, and the energy from her anger arrived a split second before she appeared. Immediately, she began hitting me with what seemed to be all of the hatred in her heart. Her fists fell all

18

over my face, and I counted at least 20 times that she administered blows we commonly refer to as haymakers in boxing.

She called out everything that was wrong with my outburst. As I felt a fist to my eye, she said, "You're disrespectful; you have an attitude, and you think you bad, don't you?" Another fist on my lip. "Well, I'm badder than you, and Imma show you today just how bad I am," she continued.

The beating continued for about 30 to 45 seconds. Blood ran down my face, but I just couldn't move; I didn't cry or say one word to my mother because I was completely empty inside.

I accepted the beating, but at that moment, I released her from all responsibilities to me as a mother. Even at that age, I decided a child should not be in such an environment, and I wanted out by any means necessary. At this moment, my survival skills met and married my physical body, and I was introduced to my "old" soul. That same soul that lives with me today and has guided me ever since that moment. It was the moment my divorce from oppression, guilt, terror, low self-esteem, and self-hatred became finalized. I decided, at the age of 13, not to hate myself simply because someone else does—even if it was my own mother!

What's The Big Secret?

My birth father was never there to protect me. I don't know much about Curtis Smith or his family, but I respect the fact that my presence in this reality is due to his genetic contribution–but that is about all I know about him. I am not even sure if paternity was established at the time of my birth, so I honestly cannot say he is my true father.

I've only had one conversation with my father as an adult, and that interaction completely deflated my self-esteem and motivation to have more.

I was visiting my friend Wanda in Atlanta for the Christmas break during my Junior year of college. I decided to get married and wanted to take this opportunity to connect with my father. I wanted to invite him to the wedding so he could share a great day in my life. I asked his sister, Joanne, for his number, but his family seemed very protective of his privacy and didn't relinquish information very quickly but I explained that I was getting married and desperately wanted my father to attend the wedding. Romanticizing my marriage apparently touched my aunt's heart, because she handed over the contact information to his home in Germany. But finding enough courage to call him was one of the toughest things I had to do in my life up to that point.

When I found out he lived in Germany, I didn't expect him to attend the wedding, but I hoped he would accept the offer and kindly decline, so I made the call. But what happened was not what

I expected. His wife answered the phone in a polite, soft voice. She asked for my name and placed me on hold.

Curt's voice was deep and brassy, tinged with matured softness. I introduced myself and explained who I was in detail. I imagine the shock was overwhelming for him, but I proceeded to explain the reason for my call. His response was, "what do you want me to do about that?"

I was devastated and quickly ended the conversation to save face. I now understand why he responded that way, and I would have had a hard time agreeing to attend a stranger's wedding, too. Nonetheless, my feelings were crushed, and I swore to never speak to him again.

During my visits, his family provided me with subtle historical facts about my father, but no one ever divulged information about where he lived and what his life was like. Often, I felt as if there was a secret about him that, if shared, would cause the entire family structure to collapse. I recall feeling as if I were proof of my father's covert actions, and his family was trying to protect him from me.

I can count on one hand the number of times I have visited Curt's family. I kept in contact with his brother, Uncle Kenny, the most over the years--stopping by or calling to say hello. Like my grandmother, Uncle Kenny was very cordial to me.

Curt's mother, Grandma Ruth, was always very nice to me and would make me hot biscuits whenever I did visit. She was a sweet lady who genuinely seemed to care for me--well, as much as she could since I didn't see her very often. I hoped to create my own relationship with her as an adult, but she died from Alzheimer's when I was in my twenties.

When I received word of Grandma Ruth's death, I immediately packed my bags and shoved them into my Hyundai Elantra and hit the road on a 13-hour trip to Pelham, Georgia. The trip was even longer for me because I thought about her the whole time. I was thankful for her ability to make me feel like I was part of the family even though my visits were infrequent, which was why I adored her so much. I also thought of how I would miss having someone who could connect me with my father. Many times during that trip, the thought of what it might be like to finally meet my father overwhelmed my thoughts, and I hoped he would be at the funeral. Then, I felt guilty because I sincerely and genuinely loved my grandmother and didn't want this to be the reason we would meet, but the thought of having a conversation with him would be a dream come true. I always imagined that he was a high ranking officer since my grandmother told me that he was still in the military.

When I arrived for the funeral, I asked my Uncle Kenny and a couple of my father's siblings if he had arrived, and I was shocked to learn that my father had already left to return to Germany the previous day. Hurt and disappointment overtook me, and now, my grief was for the death of my grandmother and the missed opportunity to meet my father face-to-face. I was still determined to visit with and get to know my family, but I was spinning from the impact of not seeing my father.

Just before the funeral services, while standing outside the church, I heard someone call my name. "Corey?!" the deep voice asked. I turned and said, "yes, that's me." I turned to see a tall, dark guy who was walking with a shorter, heavier dude; I guessed they were both around my age. Naturally, I thought they were distant relatives--perhaps a set of cousins I had not met. The taller of the two asked, "do you know who we are?" He said it as if I should have known, but by this time, I was hoping they would tell me and not make me guess.

"Sorry, fellas, I can't say that I do." said, "Are you Aunt Joanne sons?" I knew they weren't Aunt Joanne's sons because I'd met all of her children, but I was attempting to move the discussion along. "Nah, we ain't Joanne's sons! I'm Tony, and this is Michael," the taller of the two said. "Uncle Kenny told us to come and talk to you since we are brothers." Michael finally chimed in.

"Curtis Smith is our father, too," Michael continued. He smiled and spoke with confidence and excitement, but a million emotions danced around in my heart like aimless hippies, bumping into each other at every turn. I was excited to have another piece to the mysterious father puzzle I had been trying to solve for years. My mind immediately formed so many questions to help me better understand what was going on. I had another set of brothers—and maybe more? He said, "our" father. Did they live with him? What was their relationship with our father like? We seemed to be the same age, so there was some overlap in the timeline of when we were conceived.

Nevertheless, there was an underlying feeling of happiness. I found out through conversations that Tony and I were only four months apart, and Michael was two years younger and had lived with our father when his parents were married. He was too young to remember when our father divorced and left his mother. Despite the lack of memory, I was immediately jealous of Michael when I found out he had lived with him, and I hadn't.

We all talked for a long time and promised to stay in touch. Tony and I became closer and did exchange calls every once in a while, but eventually, our contact faded away. I learned from my new brothers that our father was a complete womanizer and didn't care about the children he left behind as a result of his uncontrollable sexual desires.

In the end, Grandma Ruth was laid to rest peacefully in the local cemetery, and I still didn't learn enough about my father or his family to understand that part of myself. Coming to terms with the fact my father never intended to know who I was, or even acknowledge my existence, left me with a horrible void in my spirit. I felt alone as if I'd been abandoned all over again. I was hurt and disappointed by his rejection.

The lack of a connection with my father damaged my confidence as much as the abuse I faced from my mother. It became a building block in the depressive fortress life was building around my success. Eventually, I packed the absence and feelings of rejection from my father into the same emotional hole I'd placed the abuse from my mother and stepfather. I stored it all in the back of my mind and used it as fuel to work harder and become more successful.

The Wolf In Sheep's Clothing

From the moment I met my stepfather, I was uncomfortable around him.

I was about five when he and my mother started seeing each other. Even at that age, I knew there was something peculiar about him. Maybe I was too young to define what I now think of as his very sneaky personality, but as I grew older, I became better equipped with personal skills to determine what it was about him that made my skin crawl.

He was a very quiet man, but let's be very clear--he was not a silent, influential father figure who guided me with choice words when I wandered off the beaten path. His silence seemed very mischievous, as if he was having dirty thoughts he had to keep private-- and the only way he could keep his secret was not to talk at all. Very often, when a person is that quiet, they're having very insightful thoughts, and when they do speak, their conversations are deep and meaningful. However, I never received jewels of wisdom from him. He was a self-proclaimed preacher, but the only sermon I heard him preach was literally only 5 minutes long!

There was something about his eyes; they were creepy and made me uneasy. They hid deep behind his eyebrows, and his forehead protruded like a Neanderthal. When he looked at you, the intensity of them seemed to be staring directly at the soul of a person. He always looked like he was ready to commit murder or rob a bank.

It wasn't my stepfather's appearance that caused me the most trauma. Instead, it was his personality and demeanor I never really connected with. Despite being soft-spoken and a "Man of God," I always felt evil energy radiating from him, and I guess I felt that way for a good reason. He had strange mannerisms and something about him that didn't align with the persona of a preacher.

For example, my stepfather had an extensive collection of pornography on video cassettes – at least 100. He kept the videos in a cabinet in their room, which remained locked all the time. As adolescent boys, my brother and I were curious about why the cabinet was locked, so eventually, we discovered how to unlock the cabinet with a flat head screwdriver.

We were not ready for what we found.

The variety of his collection was as creepy as his demeanor.

It seemed that our discovery and the presence of so much porn coated our house in a dirty, shameful film. It followed me like an ugly cloud that took me years to escape. Although I was never sexually abused by my stepfather, finding his porn collection at such an early age compromised my sexual innocence. Our curiosity overrode our innocence, so we watched in wide-eyed wonder.

As a result, my brother and I became sexually desensitized, which, ultimately, lead to early sexual behavior. The traumatic experience of discovering a full library of porn at a very young age was made worse by the mental and physical abuse my brother and I received.

In retrospect, I can understand why my stepfather seemed to have no problem with being so physically abusive of my brother and me. When you watch unspeakable torture on film, it is easy to behave as if it is normal. The cruelty showed up in the way he treated us.

I remember one day, I was told to go with my stepfather to the local hardware store. When we got there, he purchased two long chains, about 6 feet long. He also purchased 4 "u" shaped door handles and padlock and a box of screws.

As will any curious child, I asked, "whatcha doin' with that?" He only replied, "be quiet, you'll see." Immediately, his evil energy filled the car, to the point that it made me feel physically ill and exhausted.

When we got home, he walked directly to his toolbox and grabbed the power drill set. Burning with curiosity and fear, I asked again, "whatchu about to do?" With more frustration and anger in his voice than before, he said, "go sit down before I get that belt."

He drilled one door handle on each of the four sides of the refrigerator and looped the chains underneath the handles and crossed them over the top of the fridge, and placed a padlock through the ends. I was in shock! Right before my very eyes, and with my help, he had locked away food to prevent my brother and me from eating! That was one of the most traumatic events I experienced in my entire life.

From that point on, we were only allowed to touch that refrigerator when he, or my mother, was home.

Now, I understand growing boys will devour food at a rate that can make parents frustrated, but feeding them is part of the responsibilities parents sign up for when they have children. In his case, he signed up when he decided to marry my mother!

But I wish that was the only thing he did to make me question his sanity. Once, I witnessed his complete brutality when the family dog, Caesar, decided to make a meal of my stepfather's chickens.

The incident happened on a Saturday. Everyone was cleaning, washing clothes, and handling other miscellaneous tasks around the house when my stepfather rushed into the house. He was upset about something, which immediately sent me into a fight or flight moment.

He was mumbling something about a stupid dog and asked, "where is that rope?"

I ran to the door to see what was causing the commotion, and there they were, laying all over the yard. It was the country version of a massacre; there were blood and chicken remains scattered about the yard as if Ceasar had taken some bad drugs and went berserk. I couldn't understand why Ceasar did what he did, perhaps he had rabies, but I was concerned with what my stepfather would do to him in return.

My stepfather pushed past me on the way out the door and said, "come help me."

He had some rope and matches in his hands, which brought some very terrifying thoughts and questions into my head. He said to me, "grab him" as he gestured to Caesar. I could tell at that very moment that Caesar sensed he was in great trouble. His eyes had a look that screamed, "I didn't mean it, I was out of my mind, please, don't hurt me. I'm sorry."

So again, I asked, "what are you going to do?"

"You'll see," he said.

What I disliked about my stepfather the most was whenever I asked a question, he always answered with either very few words or in what seemed to be a riddle. Nevertheless, this time, I looked past his effort to be mysterious due to my great concern for my four-legged friend.

As I squatted and held Caesar, my stepfather tied one end of the rope around his neck. He tied the other end around a nearby tree. Then he said, "back up." I stood and watched, in horror, as he lit our family dog on fire. And all I could do was stand there and watch him burn as he yelled for mercy. My stepfather looked pleased with himself, wearing revenge all over his face. I imagine the look on my face matched the feelings I had inside, which were of terror, trauma, and utter disbelief. I was speechless. I couldn't move.

But the torture was not complete. My stepfather grabbed a 2x4 board from a nearby pile of wood. As Caesar ran around the tree, yelping and frantically trying to free himself, my stepfather swung the 2x4, striking Caesar as he passed him. He connected several times, but for some reason, he couldn't manage to hit Caesar in the head and put him out of his misery.

At this moment, I wanted the torture to be over. But it wasn't and Caesar would suffer even more brutality. The rope broke because the fire had seared it into the flesh around his neck. Seeking relief, he ran underneath the house, which caused a huge panic because he was still on fire and could burn down the whole house.

My stepfather chased after him and used a longboard to get Caesar from underneath the house. Luckily, the flames finally went out, but he was still in pain. Caesar barked and whimpered helplessly. After about 5 minutes of my stepfather poking him with the longboard, Caesar finally ran from beneath the house and disappeared into the nearby woods. I stood still, petrified and traumatized from what I had just witnessed.

The cruel and torturous killing of our family dog was not justified by what he had done the night before. My stepfather could have put Caesar to rest humanely, not in the harsh and very unusual method that had taken place.

For far too many reasons to count, my stepfather's behavior made me wary, and I did not trust him. I had always sensed his darkness, and the energy of his sadistic thoughts horrified me as a child. My intuition proved to be correct, unfortunately, and I have suffered tremendously because of the trauma inflicted by that man.

The Trauma: I struggled with trusting the people around me until I was well into my twenties. I always felt that if I couldn't trust my "parents," I couldn't trust anyone. And, because I had witnessed such sadistic acts coming from the people who were supposed to protect me, I thought everyone else must operate in such a manner, too. And since all I'd been exposed to was dysfunctional behavior, this madness was normal to me! Reversing the dysfunction and addressing my anger and self-esteem problems took time and a great deal of mental and emotional strength.

The Learning Point: Because of the emotional and mental trauma my brother Tommy and I were exposed to, I now have a stronger mentality than most of my peers, and I'm somewhat wiser than them. I knew early in life that there is no excuse for such behavior, but I am a stronger person because I have witnessed such horrific acts.

My **spiritual** connection to God and the world was greatly diminished and almost broken after witnessing the torture of our family dog. Even after all the cruelty bestowed upon me and Tommy, I remained spiritually connected to my surroundings. But seeing the horror in another living creature's eyes as I had on the day of Caesar's torture, compromised my connection with nature; I couldn't feel the liveliness from my surroundings anymore. **Mentally**, I could not make sense of the abuse, the deprivation of food, or the early exposure to sex. I created barriers to deal with my mental anguish. I couldn't understand why I experienced such violence, but I was determined to heal myself and move on.

Abuse

I was around ten years old when I witnessed Tommy, be abused at the hands of my parents.

We were at a relative in-law's house while my mom and stepfather were at work. There was a nearby store where all the kids would go for candy and other treats.

Aunt Tonya asked Tommy and me to go to the store. Tommy, is a wily character and tends to do as he feels without thinking about the consequences.

When we got to the store, he wanted a soda to drink, but we were only given enough money for the item we had to buy. But Tommy didn't care that we didn't have enough money, and, before I realized what happened, Tommy opened the cold case, grabbed a soda, and started drinking.

So, now there was a dilemma: do we get the item we were sent to the store for, or pay for the soda? Because Tommy was the oldest, he ultimately made the decision. He paid for the item, but when the cashier asked for more money to cover the drink, we had to confess that we couldn't cover it. The cashier was angry and relentlessly demanded more money, but we couldn't produce it out of thin air.

The store clerk contacted Aunt Tonya, who rushed over immediately and provided the meager 50 cents for the soda. The cost of the soda wasn't the issue, but the fact that Tommy had opened and drank in the store knowing he didn't have the money for it was. She took us home, fussing the entire way back. I wasn't afraid of her, but

I was terrified of what my mother and stepfather would do when they found out, and I knew Tommy was doomed.

While we waited for them to pick us up, I couldn't think of anything other than the brutal beating Tommy would receive. I was truly scared for him.

When my parents got back, Aunt Tonya told them what happened, and immediately, my mother became infuriated. Her yelling was quickly followed by extreme threats to "beat the badness" out of Tommy. As we were riding home, my mother asked Tommy why he opened the soda and drank it knowing he didn't have money to pay for it. He surprised me when he admitted, "I did it to hurt you!"

Tommy's reply will forever be stuck in my memory because it was bold, weird, and very accurate. And, although I was three years younger than Tommy, I knew his decision to respond in that manner was very stupid because that comment sent my mom over the top. She yelled even louder, spewing threats uncontrollably.

As soon as we arrived home, my mother sent Tommy to the bedroom. Mom's anger caused her to move aggressively through the house as she searched for something. When she found a thick leather belt, she stormed into the room, where Tommy was waiting in fear. As she drew back to swing the thick leather strap, Tommy instinctively, and out of fear, reached out and grabbed the belt. As if that wasn't enough, he wouldn't let go, causing her to become even angrier. She told him to let go repeatedly, but he wouldn't.

Frustrated beyond her limit, she bolted from the room and went thundering down the narrow hall, sounding like a bull in a china shop. She scurried throughout the house, yelling for our step dad to help her, and he gladly obliged her request.

He stood at the door as to guard Tommy's escape, while she searched for something. I had no clue what she was looking for, but I was not trying to be in the way of her getting to it. She mumbled and talked to herself, saying, "Oh, so you did it to hurt me, huh?! Well, I'm about to show you hurt."

After about five minutes of rummaging, she finally found the tool she would use to inflict her torture on Tommy. She was searching for a bundle of extension cords. She used four extension cords to tie Tommy's hands and feet to the bedposts while our step dad held him steady.

Tommy's horrifying screams for help pierced my body and soul. Fear traveled through every part of my body as I listened just outside of the door. I peaked in to view the scene of yet another horror story. They'd stripped him of his clothes, and he was tied to the bed like he was a wild animal that was unable to be tamed.

Tommy was beaten without regard for where they struck him with the belt. I watched as the strap landed once across his chest, and again as it cut across both his legs. Their abusive blows assaulted the entire front side of his body as he screamed for help that never came. He begged and pleaded for them to stop. They didn't.

I was completely traumatized at the sight of this live re-enactment from the Roots saga. I stood in the door, shocked and immobilized by fear as this nightmare unfolded before my eyes.

Finally, she turned to me and said, "I'm tired." She'd beaten my brother until she was thoroughly exhausted, so I can't even imagine how Tommy must've felt. And, you would think the madness would end there, but it didn't. My mother reached out to hand the belt to me and said, "beat him for me." That's when the second wave of terror surged through my body.

Naturally, I was speechless and completely mortified. Why would she ask me to do it? She knew how much I loved Tommy. Why didn't she ask my stepfather to help her? Isn't that why she called him in the first place?

She said, "if you don't beat him, Imma get you next." Out of fear, immaturity, and an inability to defend myself, I obliged my mother's request. And I don't have the words to tell you how emotionally painful it was to have to hurt the only person in the entire world who had been beside me during every experience of abuse I'd ever endured.

Tommy and I were joined at the hip because we'd endured the same hell together. My heart broke into bits, and at that moment, I felt irreversibly drained of all emotion except utter sadness. And every time he begged and pleaded for me not to hit him, it broke me inside. My heart took as much of the assault as his body did. There were many days after that when I revisited this memory, and I cried for him and for me.

I suffered with my brother, and perhaps even more, because I was left feeling like a coward. I had betrayed the one person I knew for sure loved me. I was never quite the same after that.

Delayed Impact

The abuse of Tommy was a significant turning point in my life, and the trauma from that experience caused me severe mental strain that lasted far beyond the experience. I lost trust in the inherent good in people and their ability to be kindhearted and caring; it took me a long time to regain my footing and learn that everyone was not the same as my parents.

My stepfather was a preacher, and my mother was deeply involved in the church. How could two people who claimed to be God-loving, God-fearing parents inflict such unprecedented pain on their children? Is this something God would do or sanction? I understand that the Bible says, "Whoever spares the rod hates their children, but the one who loves their children is careful to discipline them". But even at that age, I realized that the brutality and the extent of that beating was nothing less than evil.

Because of that horrifying experience, I have become a self-appointed protector of children who are being mistreated, abused, or neglected in any way. I have also become a powerful advocate for the overall health and wellbeing of children everywhere. Actually, I'm a protector of anyone who is in need because those feelings are an unfortunate reminder of my past, and I'm sometimes troubled by how it's still impacting my life some 30 years later.

My instincts are so keen that I sometimes forget to separate what is happening at this moment from what I experienced as a child, and that has gotten me into some pretty compromising situations.

One such incident took place on another hot, Summer Saturday. My son's fifth-grade football team was in the fourth quarter of what we considered a routine game. In Texas, kids start playing football very young and are serious about their development as players. Because I made a strong commitment to myself to be as involved as possible in my kids' lives, I coached his team. The team was outstanding; we were number one in the league and loaded with great athletes. And because of our unparalleled talent, we easily annihilated our opponents.

During this particular game, we were up thirty-six to zero, and our offense had the ball midfield and lined up for a run play on second and ten. One of our star running backs caught a pitch from the quarterback and bolted to the left edge. There was one player between the running back and the wide-open field, with one block to free him from the pursuing defender. One of our young, dominant linemen came from nowhere and put the defender on his back. The running back's speed kicked in and off he went into the horizon.

We teach our athletes to block until the play is over, so the lineman did just that. When the defender got off the ground, he put him right back on his butt. I would have liked for our player to show a bit more sportsmanship, but on a play where the running back was off to the races, this play was perfectly legal.

The referee stood just six feet away from the play and observed the entire interaction. No flags were thrown, and there were no hand gestures to let us know there was a penalty forthcoming. However, the play must not have sat well with the opponent's coaching staff, because a huge man bolted onto the field and made a mad rush in the direction of our lineman.

Without thinking, I ran onto the field. As I moved in their direction, he rushes for the referee instead. Apparently, he disagreed with the ref's interpretation of the play. At that point, I relaxed and moved back to our sideline while keeping an eye on the maniac.

I watched as his emotions quickly grew out of control. In a matter of seconds, the wild guy was yelling and pointing his finger just half an inch from the referee's face. He pushed the referee to the ground and stormed toward our lineman. I was on the field immediately, but not before I watched this out of control tyrant push our eleven-year-old player to the ground! Our athlete got up immediately and started walking toward our sideline, crying, as this grown man shoved him forward as if to say, "get over there, now!"

That was when I completely lost control of myself. I was so angry, all I saw was red.

Seconds after his hands left our player's back, I was lifting him in the air and forcefully threw him down onto the field's turf. This guy was about six feet four inches and weighed no less than two hundred and forty pounds, so his landing was thunderous and extremely dramatic. I don't remember much after that, but there was plenty of video footage of the event.

When I looked up, a crowd of men came rushing my way. Half of them were there to support me and calm me down, and the other half wanted to ensure I didn't severely hurt this guy. And the more everyone tried to subdue me, the angrier and stronger I became. I tried to get my hands on this guy, but the crowd of men stood between us until I finally walked away. Two men I didn't know approached me quickly and aggressively; before I could even think about it, I delivered a reactionary punch to the faces of both men. A group of men grabbed me and quickly dragged me away from the altercation.

I was told I should leave immediately to avoid getting into trouble, so my wife took me to the car and frantically drove us home. When we arrived, she was shaking, nervous, and scared, but she still tried to calm me. I love her for that.

But I should've stayed at the scene because six months later, the police served me a warrant to appear in court. I was charged with two counts of assault for the punches I delivered to those two men at the game. I had never been in trouble prior to this incident other than a couple of speeding tickets. I was nervous because I knew this could affect my successful and somewhat public career.

I still believe I was right for defending our player from that crazy man, but my uncontrollable anger also caused me two charges and a lot of money that impacted my family's livelihood.

I was confident the judge would sympathize with me and drop my case since this was my first offense, but I was wrong. The judge had very little sympathy. After almost ten thousand dollars in lawyer fees and court costs and a stint of community service, my case would be closed, but not before I participated in anger management classes.

I couldn't believe it! Sure, I was sometimes explosive, but I wasn't angry! I've always considered myself to be a very spiritual guy, I was like a Black Mahatma Gandhi, dammit! How could I need anger management classes? I did yoga and meditated to ensure my emotional state is always balanced, and I did everything I could to stay centered. I was no savage! I read Eckhart Tolle, Sadguru, and Mooji. I understood life very well, and the safety and peacefulness of others is almost always what drives my actions. So why would the judge order me to complete eight hours of anger management classes? I thought, "she is crazy for sure."

It was the mandated anger management that made me most upset, but those sessions would prove to change my perspective and greatly improve my spiritual life. Those classes helped me understand how my past abuse traumatized me and caused misinterpretations of my mental health as being normal and under control. So, although I disagreed with her order, I promptly started my sessions.

Kim, my counselor, was an unassuming, slender lady who wore her hair short and natural that was close to her scalp. Her manner was stiff, and her attire was somewhat eclectic which always varied in shades of purple, blue, and red. Aside from her interesting attire, she was very laid back and emitted positive energy. She smiled tenderly as she observed my demeanor during our first session. The questions she asked were as basic and structured as I imagined they would be. In fact, the first six sessions were somewhat mundane and routine. The end of the seventh session is what caused my mental and spiritual paradigm shift.

As the counselor and I continued to exchange questions and answers, there was suddenly a long and very dramatic pause; the atmosphere became somewhat awkward and uncomfortable. We stared at each other intensely, both of us deep in our own thoughts. I wondered what she was thinking and if she was going to recommend more counseling sessions. I wanted these sessions to be over, so my fear grew as the silence continued. I imagined she was thinking about how she could help me release the trauma I experienced as a young man.

We closed the session, and as I began to pack my things, she cleared her throat as if she had something to say. She'd become fed up with my robotic demeanor and short responses. She sighed loudly and said, "Corey, listen to me - God hasn't broken you yet."

Confused, I responded immediately, "What do you mean by 'broken' me?" I had been through unimaginable mental, physical, and emotional abuse for years. I had lived on the streets and with other people's families to survive. How can I possibly not be broken yet? I couldn't understand why she would say that to me, especially after I explained, in great detail, all the abuse and neglect I had overcome.

Kim noticed my agitation and immediately apologized for catching me off guard with her statement, but she still insisted that her observation was correct. I left that session feeling severely depressed and angry.

I went home and sat on my couch, literally, all weekend. I didn't eat, and I hardly talked with my family. My ten-year-old son noticed a shift in my energy and gently placed his hand on my back. He looked in my eyes and asked if I was okay. I wasn't. It was obvious that her statement deeply impacted me, but I had no idea what she meant or what to do with all of the feelings it stirred up inside of me.

I wondered why Kim would think I could be any more broken than I already felt. The more I insisted that I was fine just as I was, the further into a downward spiral I went.

Every emotional pain I felt the day I watched and participated in Tommy's brutal beating found its way back into my stomach and chest. I struggled to breathe as sorrow placed its wicked hand over my face to suffocate me. I contemplated not returning to the final session. How could I go back and speak with a person who conjured up such strong negative emotions in me like a mad voodoo priestess? I wanted to give in to the fear, but the fighter in me would not allow me to quit. I had been a fighter up until this point, and I wouldn't stop fighting now. I resolved that I would finish the sessions—after all, there is only one left.

Instead of meeting at the library as we had for the previous seven sessions, the last meeting was at her office. Kim's office was warm and inviting. There were plants everywhere, and a big window that let in lots of sunlight. There was a big comfortable couch that I sat on across from where she was sitting at her desk, with her legs comfortably crossed at the ankle. I hesitated because the memory of the statement she made during the last session was still with me. Anger and resentment consumed me, and I struggled to fight the feeling as I took a seat. But as soon as my ass touched the cushions of the couch, all those emotions reached their pinnacle. Like the great Iguazu falls of Argentina, a steady river of tears flowed over my face as if it were eroding rocks. The river flowed uncontrollably, and I cried hysterically for what seemed to be twenty minutes with no ability to speak. I tried to talk but gagged on tears and the weight of those emotions. I took deep breaths to regain my composure. I wondered whether she was judging me, but she said nothing as she sat and watched this grown man crying. She assured me that she wasn't judgmental saying that I should take my time and let the emotions flow. Suddenly, I knew this was what she meant by being broken. She reminded me of the need for me to stay with my feelings and be in the moment.

So, there I was, trying to regain my composure and talk out what had gotten me to the point of crying like a lost child trying to find the love of his mother. That's when I realized what led to those emotions.

Because I'd been thinking about the abuse I had endured, I was able to acknowledge how difficult it was to get over that pain. At one point over that long, depressive weekend, I relived the dreadful experience of seeing Tommy bound to the bed, bleeding and begging to be released, only to have more abuse inflicted upon him by me. I felt guilty for contributing to my brother's pain. I recalled the eye bleed caused by my mother's back hand.

I sat there in front of the counselor breathing deeply and tried to get back to being the collected person she saw during the first seven sessions. I thought I had myself under control, but every time I thought about Tommy, I cried some more.

She said absolutely nothing to me to provoke that reaction. Those emotions were always there, just below the surface of my psyche. Allowing myself to feel them was like having a red-hot knife slowly pushed into my chest cavity,searing my heart and filling it with sorrow. I mean, I couldn't stop crying, and the pain grew deeper the more I cried. And the more I tried to gain control over my emotions, the further away from being in control I got.

Kim finally said, "Let it go, Corey. Crying is exactly what you need to do. It doesn't make you weak. You've already held it longer than you should've, and you need to release this deep pain. You'll feel better if you do, I promise."

After forty-five minutes of deep sobbing and mucus-filled mumbling, I finally regained control. And she was right; I felt better. I felt like the knife was removed from my chest and the burning had subsided. Someone had removed the emotional shackles from my ankles that had held me in bondage for thirty-plus years. I decided to remain in counseling and keep working on my emotions; I realized many valuable lessons about myself over the months following that session.

The first thing I realized was that I was very good at compartmentalizing my emotions and denying the impact of my traumatic experiences. Being hurt so much as a child, I had a lot of practice putting my feelings away in the back of my mind like winter clothes in early Spring. Instead of dealing with them, I had become hyper-focused on achieving my life goals at all costs. I would be successful by my own definition. I was determined to change and have a successful family life. I would not repeat the history I fought to overcome. But, my ability to compartmentalize my emotions caused me to push the people who cared for me the most away because of my fear of conjuring up those past emotions.

Working Through Abuse

The thing about surviving abuse is that I always felt guilty and ashamed of what had happened to me, even though I knew that it really had nothing to do with me. My mother was an angry and aggressive woman for as long as I could remember, she never needed a reason for yelling at us. The yelling, I imagine, is common with many mothers. But the physical abuse that accompanied it was specific to few houses, as far as I knew. So, as a child, I thought I was the cause of her pain and frustration. I was just too young to understand otherwise, so I began to blame myself and felt guilty whenever they beat me.

Even well into my young adult years, I continued to blame myself for living in that toxic environment. At that point in my life, there was no one to explain that the abuse was not my fault. And as the guilt grew, thoughts of being a 'bad' child became normal. I started to think everything I did was bad. Chronic self-doubt consumed me. So, I withdrew into myself for a while and became afraid to speak to teachers and other students. I had no way of knowing these feelings were the result of the physical and mental abuse I endured.

The neglect further punctuated my self-doubt. My brother and I were left to fend for ourselves many times, which kept me in a state of chronic loneliness.

One particularly lonely memory took place in 1985, when Kate, a Category 3 Hurricane, touched down, bringing winds up to 100 miles an hour with her. Tommy was thirteen, and I was nine; it was just one day before my tenth birthday. We were home alone when the weather warnings started showing on the television. In Georgia, many homes are built off the ground using concrete blocks, so they're somewhat vulnerable during hurricane season. So, there we were, two kids home alone during a severe storm that was growing more violent by the minute. I can still remember the house shaking like that scene from The Wizard of Oz. We were scared, and rightfully so!

My brother and I crawled through the house on our hands and knees to find what we considered the safest place to wait out the storm until we heard an even louder boom of thunder that sent us looking for a safer place. We endured that storm together, and because of it, our bond became stronger; but my mother and stepfather were not there to comfort us during this terrifying experience.

The following year, almost to the date, my brother and I were left home alone again. Only this time, it was Thanksgiving! How did we get left behind during a family holiday like Thanksgiving?! My mother and stepfather had two children together, and they all were at "Big Mommas" house. But my brother and I were left to fend for ourselves.

Tommy, always the provider and protector, was boiling some turkey wings so we could have our own Thanksgiving dinner, and I wouldn't feel so bad about being left home. When we heard a car pull up outside, we rushed to the window with excitement and anticipation, thinking it must be our mother returning so she could take us to Big Momma's house with everyone else. Instead, it was Leticia a cousin of our stepfather getting out of the car and walking toward the house. She came in and told us to get dressed. I remember the look on her face seemed to be disappointment mixed with sincere empathy. She was sad for us because she had just come from Big Momma's and she knew our mother had no intention of picking us up so we could enjoy the holiday with the family.

Early in life, I had to let go of the expectation of having a loving mother to nurture and nourish me. We received discipline, but we never received love. Discipline, when given correctly, should help a child grow into a more responsible citizen of their community and the world. But discipline does not equal physical, emotional, or mental abuse. I knew that what I was experiencing was not love. It was, in fact, the opposite of love. I lived in an environment of hate.

There are many examples of abuse, neglect and poverty. Thinking back on my childhood, I realize that I'd received very few birthday or Christmas presents. I vaguely remember a hand full of times where I received clothes for school. The poverty was so common where I grew up, it felt normal.

I always tried to understand if I was the blame for the treatment and, if so, how. I wondered whether I was even worthy of being loved. A profound sadness lived in me throughout my childhood and remained embedded in my heart well into my adolescence and young adult life.

I often felt belittled by my mother and stepfather, and the physical abuse made me timid and afraid to be myself. No one seemed to like me, not even my mother and that became the foundation of my negative self-image. Finding the courage to push through and succeed in life was a very daunting road to travel for anyone in my condition, but I persevered.

Spiritual Maturity

I was reasonably tall and muscular as a young male. Most kids in rural settings are physically stout due to the physical work that is commonly attached to farm life.

One day, I was supposed to feed and give water to my stepfather's massive pet rabbits--all 50 of them. But, as young boys will do from time to time, I failed to finish my chore, and in my house, that came with grand repercussions. My mother was deeply annoyed whenever one of us did not complete the tasks we were assigned, and based on how I was raised, it was unthinkable for the children of the home to skip them altogether. It's not unusual for a kid to have to be reminded a couple of times, but in our house, being reminded at all was unacceptable.

My mother was furious as she stormed into the house and immediately yelled, "Why haven't you finished feeding the rabbits?"

I softly spoke out, "I'm sorry, um, um…" I quickly tried to reply in the best way I could.

It was common in my house to apply physical violence during times of frustration and disappointment. So, my mother balled her fists up and hit me a couple of times in the face.

A sudden jolt of testosterone caused me to have a knee-jerk reaction, and I responded, "don't hit me no more!"

But I was quickly slapped back to reality by my mother as she responded, "Who do you think you're talking to?"

That question was followed by a couple more punches to the face and a barrage of words that said, "I don't care how big you're getting, you don't talk to me that way."

But the shift was complete at that point, and I felt committed to ending the violence and slave-like mental hold over me that my mother was attempting to maintain.

So, I responded, "I'm tired of you hitting me all the time," as I stormed straight into the room I shared with my older brother.

My mature and masculine moment didn't last long, because my mother followed me and busted through the door like S.W.A.T. She told me to get off the bed. I stood up and leaned my back against the dresser facing out towards my mother.

This time, she was filled with uncontrollable anger ten times greater than ever before. Her blood-filled eyes spoke to me, saying, "I-am-completely-enraged-and-hurt-and-I-feel-totally-disrespected.

So like many times before, the punches proceeded, and her yelling accompanied.

"You're not gonna talk to me like that; I'm the parent of this house," she shouted.

For those of you who have never gotten a beating from your parents, even thirty seconds of physical abuse seems like a very long time. I can imagine that, at that point, my mom felt threatened. She felt as if she was losing control over me as an authority figure. Maybe she thought I wouldn't listen to her any longer because I was becoming a man, and my size would override the control she had over me when I was younger. There was probably fear that I might one day strike her back, but that wasn't the case. I just didn't want to be hit anymore.

I was always a mannerable child who always did what I was told, so she would have gotten the same results she wanted by merely talking to me. I felt as if the beatings were unnecessary when other kinds of punishment would work just as effectively.

When her fist made its way to my face and struck my eye, I felt the power of her anger surging through her entire being. It traveled from her shoulder, down through her elbow, and past her wrist until it jolted out of her knuckles and hit me squarely in my eye.

Even as a child, that anger said to me, "I have every right to beat you." It also said, "I don't care about you enough to be patient and teach you wisdom. Instead, I will punish you by whipping your ass, the way my parents whipped mine."

I immediately identified that moment as a period where parental love can become overshadowed by personal ego. Her ego caused her to try to maintain control over me through fear. Anger, frustration, resentment, and an inflated ego, had become part of my life and spirit as a result of those beatings.

So, at the very moment my mother was punching my face. I became filled with a sudden burst of clarity. I knew that if I didn't want to her hurt me again, I had a decision to make--even at a vulnerable age of 13. The decision required me to "get out at all costs," and I was prepared to pay whatever was necessary.

Surviving, at that age, was understandably difficult, but I knew I would be a basket case if I remained in such an abusive environment. So, armed with a sudden hunger to live on my own terms and a newly found consciousness that allowed me to realize I needed to make a drastic change, I decided to leave home.

When you rely on God and The Universe to order your steps, moments of trauma and horror can lead to moments of enlightenment and clarity. I know that fight or flight situations can become windows of opportunity that should be jumped through if you are going to get to the lessons and find better opportunities. Allowing myself to grow and ask for a better life outcome at the very moment I was enduring unspeakable violence has changed my life for the better, and the same ability to make a quick decision has become common for me now. It is in times of high stress and uncertainty that I remain calm enough to make sound, logical decisions. Through hurt and pain, and by becoming aligned with God and the Universe, I was jolted into a state of mental and spiritual maturity.

I made up my mind that I would leave, but I did not know how I would manage to feed myself, or where I would go, but I had made my declaration to The Universe and asked God for the courage to walk out.

Bad Experiences

~

PART-TWO

~

A Football Life Line

When I was an eighth-grader, I enjoyed playing basketball and I excelled in football. My friends and I pretended to be Lynn Swan while we tossed the football to each other at recess. One day, I noticed that there was always one coach who stood by and watched us play. At the time, I had no clue who he was, but that gentleman would change my life forever.

I later learned that he had a son in high school who played quarterback for one of the local teams. This same son would go on to become the starting quarterback for Florida State University and win the Heisman trophy and later go on to play professional basketball for the New York Knicks. He was such a good athlete that he decided to play an entirely different sport professionally. So, it's needless to say that the gentleman who watched my friends and I play football was well equipped to recognize good talent.

Football is huge in my home town, and coaches were always recruiting the next big talents in the area, but I had no interest in playing organized football. To me, it was just fun kidding around with my friends. But to the gentleman watching us, my talent was far too great to waste on pointless recess play.

"Corey, come here for a minute. Hurry, run over here, quick," he commanded sternly.

Suddenly, thoughts of being in trouble rushed into my head. I tried to think of all the things I'd done that day that might have been the reason I was being called over.

"Yeah, coach?" I responded timidly.

"You ever played football before," he asked with a more comforting voice.

"Yes, Sir. Me, Tony, and Jeremy play almost every day at recess." I responded confidently, knowing I wasn't in trouble.

"Nah boy, I mean on a team," he said with a deep southern drawl.

"Oh, no sir, I don't think I want to play for a team," I babbled as I started to turn and walk back to my friends.

"Hold up, why don't you want to play," he asked.

"Um, I just don't think I will like it, I guess," I replied quickly.

My response was based on my lack of confidence and the lack of support I expected to get from my family.

"Well, you gonna play next year in the ninth grade," he instructed with conviction.

"Nah, coach, I don't wanna play football," I responded.

"Yes, you're gonna play, and you're gonna be good," he insisted. "So, go talk to ya momma and daddy about it." And with that, he ended the brief discussion.

I headed back to my friends, confused and deep in thought. Why did Coach want me to play football? My mom and stepfather never pushed me to get involved in extracurricular activities, so I was sure they wouldn't allow it.

My friends must have been just as confused as I was because I was hit with a bunch of questions upon my return.

"Man, what did Coach want? Did you do something wrong?" Tony asked.

"Naw, he wants me to play football next year," I said with confusion in my voice.

"Man! Hell yeah, Dog, you should do it," Tony said with confidence.

"Nah, man, my mom ain't gonna let me play no damn football," I said.

"Dawg, just give it a try," Jeremy blurted out.

Because I had good support from my friends, I was committed to at least asking if I could play. And because I was driven even at that age, I begin daydreaming about going to college to become an architect. So, football quickly became the vehicle to get me into college and out of the hell in which I currently existed.

When my mom and stepfather got home that night, I had a bouncy kind of energy as I anticipated discussing with them. But part of me was nervous because I knew the chances of getting shutdown were far greater than they were of having my mom and stepfather support me. But I persisted through my doubts. I first approached my stepfather because, well, he was a man and might enjoy the idea of me playing a sport.

"Hey Charlie, Imma go to college," I said with boyish pride and confidence.

"How you gonna do that," he responded with a rather careless tone.

"Imma play football and get a scholarship," I boasted.

"Hahahahahahaha...yeah right," he said, clearly insulting me.

His response cut my pride and excitement like a sharp laser beam through soft plastic. His response made me feel confused and determined at the same time. Although I anticipated his response being negative, I never thought he would be that direct and degrading. My confusion and disappointment quickly turned into determination, anger, and a strong desire to prove him wrong.

"I'm gonna do it, just watch," I said with a tone that was borderline disrespectfully.

"Yeah, I don't know how you gonna do that...hahahaha," he continued to chuckle.

"A Coach asked me to play next year...so can I?" I responded sharply.

"How you gonna get back and forth to practice?" he asked, totally disengaged. And, based on his energy, I knew he meant that he was not going to be the one to take me. But I persisted in trying to get my way.

"Can you take me?" I asked.

My mom didn't drive and had no license at the time, so it was pointless asking her to support my new dreams and aspirations.

"I can't be taking you back and forward to no practice, but if you can find a way, be my guest," he said with complete dismissal in his voice.

I should have felt demoralized and deflated at this point, but because I anticipated a lack of support, I just shrugged my shoulders and said okay. I walked away, focused and determined to make this happen.

Eventually, I began to understand and deeply resent the cruelty I was exposed to. I always resented the cruelty to an extent, but the resentment grew deeper into my spirit. Thankfully, my connection to something greater gave me the courage to stand up to the hate instead of becoming equally hateful. That connection allowed me to leave that environment even though I didn't have the means to provide for myself completely. Through that connection, I began to understand what can happen to your soul when your environment is toxic, and I desired something else for myself. I wanted love, joy, and happiness, and I knew I would not find it where I was, so it was an easy decision to leave home.

~

The Time to Leave

It was customary for some of my stepfather's family to visit on Sundays after church for dinner. So, the Sunday immediately following the episode of my mother punching my face, I saw an opportunity and decided to take it. That Sunday, Alan, my stepfather's younger brother, his girlfriend, and their three daughters were visiting. We had dinner and talked, as usual, but soon everyone began to say their goodbyes in preparation for the work and school day that followed. So, knowing I needed to act quickly, I asked my stepfather's younger brother if I could go with them. Confused, he looked at his girlfriend and said, "we're going home."

I quickly and desperately responded, "I know, but can I come stay with you guys?"

Even more confused, he responded, "Don't you have school tomorrow?"

Without giving any thought to the statement, I blurted, "I know, I can walk." Even though the school was about 4 miles from where they currently lived, I was desperate and willing to do anything to escape my future demise.

My mother looked even more confused. My stepfather looked irritated and angry. My brother's eyes gleamed as if he understood my tactics. However, none of them said a word against me leaving.

Finally, Alan said, "Um, I don't care."

I quickly ran to the kitchen to grab a trash bag for my belongings because we didn't have luggage. I sprinted to the room, desperate to hurry up before everyone changed their minds, and I was scared to death that my mother would come raging in to hit me again. Shaking, I stuffed the few clothes I owned into the sack, bolted out the door, and jumped into the back seat of the Buick Riviera. The few minutes that I waited in the car seemed like hours. The life decision I was making started to sink into my spirit, and I became nauseous. But I knew I had to press on.

I walked out of my mother and stepfather's house with a trash bag full of beat up and severely used clothing over my shoulder, and she said nothing. My mother didn't say one word to convince me that she loved me or ask me to stay. Her eyes were empty, but I felt her heart must be even more empty if she would allow me to go live with another family who had absolutely no resources to take care of me. At that moment, my anxiety and fear became sadness and depression. To me, this moment confirmed that my mother didn't love me and that she had no desire to have me in her life. That experience delivered a powerful message about life .

Learning Point 1: You can't always expect people to care about you, even your own family and parents. Humans are the most intelligent animals on the planet, but they still desire family and friends to care about them. But in the grand scheme of life, they honestly don't have to care about you! Nobody is obligated to care for you, despite popular belief. At that moment, I decided to care for everyone who needed to be nurtured and loved, regardless of my relationship with them. I understand that not everyone wants to be cared for and loved, so respect is also necessary. Since that moment, I have had the opportunity to live my life from a place of pure love for everyone. I don't like many people, but I try hard to love them all!

Learning Point 2: I learned to take care of myself and develop maturity after deciding to leave that abusive environment. Thirteen is the beginning of adolescence, but that was the moment I became a young man. However, being on my own at a young age, going to live with a young family who already had three children to take care of, forced me to accept being 100% responsible for myself. I realized I had been responsible for quite some time, but now the reality of being on my own was setting in. Immediately, I began to think about things in a very real way. How would I feed myself? How would I make money so that I could live? How would I get to school? Oh shit, what the hell did I just do?!

I had to buckle down to ensure that my schoolwork remained a priority because having parents to guide me did not exist for me. The hustle had officially begun.

~

Surviving

The time I spent outside of that abusive household and taking care of myself was one of the most impactful learning periods of my life. Surviving, with no parental guidance since the age of thirteen will accelerate anyone into adulthood. To me, this was the equivalent of teaching someone to swim by throwing them into the deep end of the pool. It's sink or swim, and I had to figure out how to swim quickly. And it was at this point in life that I had to become creative about how to provide the essentials of life for myself.

Becoming good at bartering for the things I needed taught me how to find resources from the most unexpected places; it became an art form after a while, but it took me some time to get it right.

I would couch surf if possible--which meant I would stay at a different person's home for a short time, sleeping on their couch, or in any space available, before moving on to the next place. When that friend or family member grew tired of me, I would spin the story once again, cycling through all the couches available to me. I had a system, and I made it work.

For food, I ate at school. I forged the school documents that allowed me to receive free breakfast and lunch. I would put extra food in my book bag and save it for later to have some dinner. One year during high school, I failed to complete the paperwork in time, and I didn't get free lunches, so I just used the same methods to acquire the money I needed for meals. I got along with everyone, so that increased the pool of resources.

"Hey Tim, lemme get fifty cents, man!"

"Jessica, you're a cheerleader, you shouldn't drink chocolate milk. Let me take it off your hands."

I'm sure I got a reputation of being a beggar, but hey, a brother had to eat. Unfortunately, I was in a position where I had to beg for food and a place to sleep to survive, and I don't downplay this fact. But now, I'm an expert at finding available resources and asking for the budget I need to accomplish personal and company goals. These characteristics have helped label me as a leader and an influencer. I was a beggar; now, I'm a "go-getter!"

I became comfortable with asking for resources. Years later, when I started working in corporate America, my peers had to build the courage to ask for resources while I, on the other hand, felt quite comfortable with asking for what was needed. Even if it was for out-of-the-box, pet projects that weren't in the company's plan, I felt no stress because I was used to asking around until someone felt obliged to support. Luckily for me, most of my projects were home runs, further solidifying my reputation as a go-getter.

Now, unfortunately, I attempted to sell drugs to make money but realized very quickly that I didn't have the stomach to operate in a world that preyed on people with dependencies. Despite the lack of guidance, I chose to put what was morally right and the needs of others before my own. I believed there was a better way because I was creative; I quickly became a superb storyteller, and I used those skills to help me survive.

So, I had no job, no transportation, and no guaranteed place to call home. But I realized that I did have a skill I might be able to use to make money. My older brother sacrificed his appearance and safety and allowed me to practice being his barber for about a year. By that time, my skills were good enough for me to make a little money, but I needed customers that would like what I did enough to pay me.

I became an excellent salesman. My first cut was free, so I could showcase my skills and let my customers know I was nice with the clippers. And that also helped me refine my skills. The plan worked, and I started getting money from cuts. I would do it cheaper than trained barbers and often would go to the customer. Life started working in my favor, but the money I made wasn't nearly enough, so I bartered for the rest of my needs. I borrowed clothes from friends (and never returned them, of course). I relied on friends to get rides to and from school, which helped tremendously. All negotiated with the promise of free haircuts.

Despite the barriers in front of me, I managed to motivate myself with little to no support from family. I had to prove my worthiness to the world, so I worked harder than all my peers. My hard work resulted in compliments from teachers and those around me, which helped dispel some of my thoughts of unworthiness over time. But since I didn't receive compliments or encouragement as a child, I didn't believe in my talents, and I certainly didn't think there was anything special about me. So, I settled into the background and did my best to stay out of life's way. I now see these behaviors as the result of post-traumatic stress disorder (PTSD) that I developed because I was abused.

To cope with the aftermath of abuse, I found it best to stay very busy, so I participated in many sports and any other activities that would keep me away from home. Maintaining positive thoughts also helped minimize some of the pain of feeling unlovable. I discovered that it was very easy to fall down the rabbit hole of sad feelings, so positive thinking was very important.

Surrounding myself with positive people also helped me focus on the future I wanted for myself instead of the pain of the moments before me. I had heard the saying, "misery loves company," so I knew that being around someone else who felt the same despair would be dangerous for both of us. Even now, I limit my exposure to anyone with a severe case of depression and loneliness for that same reason. Ultimately, these actions led to my becoming a leader and someone with a positive outlook on life.

But I still had other emotional hurdles to overcome. Because of my past, I knew I had to guard against compensating for my psychological trauma and emotional voids by filling my life with material possessions.

In my early adolescence, I believed that acquiring things would make me feel special and worthy of the attention of others who I thought were special. But the good feelings those things gave me were all temporary. As soon as the newness of those material items wore off, so did the feeling of being special. Those possessions did not address the root of my problems. I needed therapy, not clothing. Ultimately, I began to realize that the acquisition of material items caused me to damage my Life's Wealth because I didn't manage my finances wisely. With the help of therapy, I discovered that what I truly needed was love.

By this time, I was sure that my mother and stepfather didn't know how to embrace me as part of the family. Accepting that fact allowed me to look beyond them to find a more loving place to be in the world.

Although the entire experience was traumatizing and daunting, I can say that it also provided me with a set of critical concepts that have helped me succeed in life.

Problem Solving

First, I became an expert problem solver during times of immense pressure. Because I had experienced the unimaginable early in life and had to make serious life decisions to escape the perils of my mother's house , I picked up the very useful skill of critical thinking and problem-solving.

Fight or Flight

Common problems and issues did not easily trigger my panic button. I viewed what most people considered a tragedy as an opportunity to change or create something better. My fight or flight reaction was present, but it took something unthinkable to cause me to take flight.

Are Inevitable

PART-THREE

Spades & Crochet

How They Changed My Life

My athleticism seems to be an irrefutable opinion shared by many. I have the stature of an athlete, so I believe it's in my blood. All the men in my family look like Zulu warriors, but none of them have ever consistently lifted weights or worked on their physical appearance

Early in my life, I discovered my natural talent for playing football. What I was able to do on the field was effortless, and quite honestly, I did it without much thought. Although I performed exceptionally well on the football field, I had a particular affinity for basketball. As a sophomore, on the basketball court is where I forged a friendship that would be the ultimate paradigm shift in my life. At the time, I was only —five feet and eleven inches tall. I was not very tall for a basketball player. My stature was more suited for football, so I didn't get much playing time. But that didn't matter much, because that's where I met Wayne Rawlings.

Wayne and I became very good friends because we played basketball together. We started hanging with each other sporadically at first, then daily--until finally, we become inseparable. He was a cool dude who seemed to sense that I was a troubled kid with a very unstable home situation.

His older sister, Wanda, was the manager of a pizza chain. After school and when we played home games, Wayne and I would frequent that pizza joint for "oops" pizzas or any free food. At the time, nobody knew that this would often be the only meal I had that day. Wayne lived with his mother Janette in a quaint three-bedroom home in a local housing project. They were a family I would place at the top of the "poor" hierarchy, and I was slowly becoming a regular in their family setting.

To be very clear, Aunt Janette saved me from an abusive, demoralizing, and troubled existence. She pulled me into the embrace of her family and their home. She didn't have much in the way of material possessions, and based on American standards, she was broke. Aunt Janette would ask probing questions that made you think, but her questions would never cut deeply enough to stir up the kind of pain and discomfort that couldn't be overcome.

The Rawlings family was huge; there were so many uncles, aunts, and cousins who would visit--bringing food and laughter with them. This kind of family life was completely foreign to me, but I loved being invited to participate in it. It was no secret that I loved Aunt Janette. I am forever grateful and appreciative of her pulling me from the grip of abuse because I was emotionally and mentally raw. I could not sit still and would often get into mischief. Wayne kept my mind busy enough to keep out of trouble, but he was only a year older than me and was heading to the military soon, leaving me in the care of his mom. So, to keep me focused, Aunt Janette needed to occupy my time with something creative and fun.

Once Wayne left for the military, it was just the two of us. On those school nights when I got an itch to go out and do something crazy, she would bring my focus to playing spades. Head to head; there were just the two of us playing a game that is the epitome of competition, and boy was I competitive.

Aunt Janette was a masterful card player, and her game of choice was Spades. Spades is the cousin to Bid Whist and Eucher, which are both book-taking card games.

The game of spades is part luck, but mostly skill. You must surrender to and work with whatever hand you are dealt (if you aren't trick dealing). Sounds a lot like life, huh? But you need skills if you're going to play well and win. You have to pay attention to the cards that have already been played. Play the wrong card at the wrong time, and the book belongs to your opponent. Because of my competitive nature, I was committed to beating her at least half the time. So, for hours, we would sit and play spades until I became an expert Spades player. And if you don't believe me, you can certainly try me, but you don't want those problems in your life – trust me.

But Aunt Janette had an even more significant strategy in mind that I had yet to realize. Auntie used Spades as a metaphor for the game of life. She intended for me to focus on learning new skills and avoid mischief. I gained the ability to focus on things that brought me joy in life as a result of playing spades with Aunt Janette.

Auntie always crocheted, too. She loved it and couldn't get enough of coming up with intricate designs for her work. Crocheting was the way she preferred to spend her downtime, and she did not want to be bothered when she did it. As I observed her creating these lovely blankets for all the people in her life, I realized the amount of strategy required to create the final product. So, Aunt Janette used my natural curiosity as another opportunity to keep me "out of the streets," and persisted in teaching me to crochet. And I was pretty good at it, although I believed this to be extremely degrading because of my macho football persona. Overall, learning to crochet was a pretty positive experience.

I particularly enjoyed learning the strategic aspect of crocheting. Now, I can equate that process with any corporate-level planning strategy where you have to consider how much time to allocate to a project. Being able to estimate the materials and how much money it will take to complete a project before you engage is important. Auntie taught me all the critical aspects of planning out a crocheting project. She would repeatedly discuss the process whenever we started a new design. Mostly, she proved to me that it was necessary to build in points at which you perform quality checks that allow you to exit before you are too far in to change course or abandon the project altogether.

Through teaching me spades and crocheting, Auntie demonstrated good parenting skills. And, because she intended for me to stay out of trouble, she was patiently stern with me about learning the best techniques. As usual, there were lessons within the lesson. For example, she taught me that, whether playing spades, building a business, or planning your life, it is imperative to take your time and be patient with yourself when creating a winning strategy. She used the same approach when finding ways to redirect my desire to go out and get into trouble.

There are very few teen aged boys who would be overly excited about learning to crochet, but Auntie encouraged me to sit still and learn the art. Because of her approach, I am incredibly comfortable with developing others through loving but stern and patient guidance. And no matter how much I protested about sitting in the house crocheting instead of being out with my friends getting into typical teenage foolishness, I am grateful that she helped me avoid mischief.

A major advantage human beings have over other mammals is our ability to create things around us that we need or want. We can bring something into existence based on our creativity, and the use of our imagination to formulate original ideas.

What I didn't realize then was how going through so many traumatic experiences as a child severely stifled my creativity. I was a brilliant kid, but because I had to take care of myself, I learned to rely more heavily on survival skills than on my innate creativity. However, Aunt Janette pushed me to embrace my creativity through the process of learning to crochet. Although I was reluctant to learn at first, imagining what new stitch I could use to create a large blanket, cap, or sweater took a great deal of imagination.

Crocheting is very relaxing and requires focus, but playing spades is fun and exciting. Auntie and I would play while exchanging harmless but witty banter to draw each other's attention away from their cards. Because of it, I developed a sharp wit and a quick tongue.

Playing spades redirected my thoughts away from my traumatic past. And because those traumatic thoughts were slowed and considerably diminished, my spiritual and mental health was improved, which increased my Life Wealth. So you see, Aunt Janette kept me occupied through simple life experiences and allowed me to be creative and learn how to have fun without getting into trouble. My ability to find joy in those simple things increased. But what would my life look like if I didn't have an open mind about learning something that didn't seem interesting to me at first?

In high school, I was an athlete, so what would I want with learning anything that required stillness? I was strong, smart, and good looking, so my popularity with the girls and the attention I received as an athlete filled the void caused by such a traumatic early life. I saw myself as a man's man, so crocheting went against all my ideas about manliness. But having an open mind allowed me to crochet well, and learning to play spades allowed me time to catch up with my peers emotionally by learning critical thinking skills and how to formulate a winning strategy. Although I was nowhere near where I needed to be socio-emotionally, by the time I graduated high school, a proper foundation had been established for me because of Aunt Janette.

The things she taught me kept my mind from dancing off into the cosmos of sorrow, pain and depression. If I focused on my past, I would have probably become extremely depressed and sad. I would have been thinking about what I did to deserve such treatment or what could have caused my mother and father not to love me. So, because thinking about my past was too painful, I thought of the future and how I would change and improve things in my life. Often, I would daydream about becoming rich and happy by dissecting undesirable future events into the steps needed to build a successful dynasty. I didn't realize that thinking so deeply about the future caused me to become anxious and frustrated. It seemed that success was not happening fast enough, if at all.

But whenever I immersed myself in devising a successful strategy for winning a game of spades or planning a complicated crochet project, thoughts of the past and future ceased to exist. For those few hours, I was never depressed, sad, or anxious. I was entirely in the now and totally without ego. I was present and filled with joy. I was comforted. I was loved.

Because I was totally focused and present, I paid more attention to Aunt Janette and the game. The peripheral thoughts of my past and future didn't cloud my awareness of the moment. I became aware of subtle gestures and micro-aggressions. Those subtleties of energy improved my ability to pay attention to how I interacted with Aunt Janette. Being present and aware of what is needed in the moment is critical to providing quality care to others. When you can have pure enjoyment without the presence of ego, you are completely present and aware of how much you care for the people around you. You begin to understand energy and your connection to everything and everyone, and you take good care of that. To me, this is the meaning of love.

College Prep with a Stranger

I found my place in a home of strangers who loved me like they had known me my entire life. Although my situation couldn't have been any more demeaning and embarrassing, it was a necessary move. Luckily, moving in with Auntie Janette, greatly improved my life.

You see, Auntie Janette worked as an aid for special needs students at my high school, so she was a strong advocate for education. Her entire family was supportive of me; they wanted to see me accomplish great things in high school and beyond. This family was a positive beam of light in my life during a very dark time.

She was especially involved in helping me prepare for college. She knew I needed to maintain my 3.6 GPA even though I worked part-time and continued to play football. She also knew how easy it would be for me to lose focus if I entertained the dark and gruesome thoughts of my past. Auntie kept me focused on my books and reminded me of how smart I was. Her formula for college success was organization. Her actions weren't huge, but they had a significant impact on every area of my life from then on.

The thought of applying to any schools--let alone several--was daunting because I was pre-occupied with my memories of abuse and regularly entertained feelings of uselessness. Although living with Auntie Jannette helped me through my depression, I still struggled to determine my best career path. But despite those mental barriers, I developed an interest in learning how to research possible schools by organizing the data and managing the information I'd gathered. And because I was responsible for doing all the work myself, I learned a lot. I performed ninety percent of the work, but Auntie Janette helped with the other ten percent. And I needed every bit of the help she offered—she mostly as a guide and a clear voice of reason.

Several universities offered me a scholarship to play football. I knew playing sports wasn't my focus, but it was a tool I would use to reach my goal of receiving a free college education. So, I had to develop even more skills if I was going to accomplish this milestone. Ultimately, I was able to identify a career path and align that with the colleges that offered me scholarships. Then I organized visits to each of those colleges to see whether they fit my expectations.

I can clearly remember my visit to Tennessee State University, which is Oprah Winfrey's alma mater, and I was amazed! For starters, I was introduced to two gorgeous women who happened to be twins! They escorted me to a fraternity party where we had a blast the entire night. Admittedly, I vaguely remember anything I heard about the football program and absolutely nothing about the architecture program, which is what I was planning to study. And that's precisely why I chose *not* to go to TSU.

I knew I had to make grown-up decisions for myself because I didn't have the luxury of parental guidance or having someone to fall back on. I knew I couldn't attend a school where I would potentially party more than I studied, so although it is a very prestigious HBCU, it was a no-go for me.

After many more campus visits and similar experiences, I narrowed my choices to a couple of schools. Now I had to determine which would be best for me from a financial perspective. And my diligence paid off because I managed to negotiate and close the deal on a one-hundred percent paid scholarship that would allow me to work with a Hall of Fame-caliber Coach and play defensive back, my preferred position. And because I did it all on my own, I knew I had developed the ability to negotiate and make good decisions based on logic and the circumstances before me. And to this day, I'm grateful that I was able to hone in on those skills and use them to position myself for the win. So, I guess I could say that the abuse I endured made me into the person I am today, and this is just another example of how I used something terrible that happened in my life to create something that would help me win in life--for the rest of my life.

It is not apparent to most of the world, but we are all connected through our energy as we go about our day to day lives. Being present and aware of your energy signature allows you to realize the connection you have with God and with everyone and everything that exists in this world. From there, the object is to venture into caring for people around you with the same awareness so you can offer a higher quality of love. Love will shine through those efforts. Aunt Janette embodied this concept. She believed that when we get to this point of balance, we ARE love.

Growth

I finally had a solid foundation of love and guidance in my life. So, instead of focusing on the negative aspects of what happened to me, I began to draw upon the vital life lessons I learned through the journey.

Through learning the game of football, I discovered that I have a relentless drive when going after something I want. So, from the time my stepfather laughed in my face until the time I played my last arena football game, I was in turbo drive mode. I have always been competitive, and I despise the idea of losing simply because I didn't prepare. So, I always prepare to win.

I set goals for myself often and will push myself to meet them as a form of self-discipline, and it is extremely self-affirming when I accomplish them. My goal-setting skills were not just for football, but for my entire life.

Success was like the main course on the menu, but if I had no money to buy it, I had to have the necessary drive to wash dishes or bus tables to get to that meal because I was determined to eat by any means necessary.

Through football, I learn the importance of teamwork. I knew that my success was highly dependent on assistance from others and allowing them to help me wherever possible. I needed a team of supporters throughout my journey to success to get me past the roadblocks. But at the time, I suffered severely from work with others.

I was considered a loner. Therefore, building my ability to work with a team became a huge priority for me.

There are eleven positions on the football field at any given time. Now, although I was a versatile player and could have probably played every position on the field, I couldn't possibly play all eleven posts at once. Despite having the athleticism to play every post, I knew I had to focus my talents on playing the position I was assigned. My job was to build the necessary skills to be the best at that position. And I had to trust my teammates to develop their skills to become the best at their jobs.

I had to lead by example as well as showcase leadership by supporting my teammates. That would prove to be a winning formula for me, and this approach led me to become the team captain in high school and college. Teamwork is like an ecosystem. Everything has a specific purpose, and if one element is flawed, the entire ecosystem is at risk of failure. I have mastered this skill so well that, even in my professional career, I have developed a reputation for helping teams perform at very high levels.

Performing at high levels in collegiate and professional settings takes an even higher commitment to developing discipline. I was able to break my approach into three key elements.

The first thing you need is passion. Passion is the foundation of all disciplines. Simply put, if you are not passionate about what you are doing, you will not develop the level of discipline needed to build skills for life or anything else, and your work ethic will be noticeably absent.

Secondly, even if you have passion, you still need to develop a plan/ strategy for maintaining your discipline. Preparing and completing the necessary actions to achieve greatness will not be easy if you are not clear on the steps needed to get there. Big picture thinking is required.

Lastly, accountability is an absolute must to maintain discipline in everything you do in life. Honestly, it is tough to hold yourself accountable, but creating reminders, notes, and phone alerts can help you become more responsible. And, as a risk management tactic, you should always have an accountability partner--someone to poke and prod you when you become discouraged.

Discipline also takes mental toughness. However, mental toughness is an element all on its own. Developing what is necessary to survive in life, thrive in sports, or achieve success in any activity you choose to participate in is usually hard. When things become too hard, human nature often tells us to give up and quit. Mentally, you have to be tough enough to say, "fuck you, failure!" and keep going anyway.

No matter how well you succeed in life, you will always have naysayers, and their negative energy is often contagious. I have always fought through the pull of their disappointing comments; they are contrary to my success.

Your journey to success will be long, and Murphy's Law is the realization of the inevitable. Murphy's Law states that "If something can go wrong, it will." To push through for the win, I had to stay positive. So I adopted what I refer to as Yphrum's Law, which is the opposite of Murphy's Law. Yphrum's law states, "whatever can work, will work." That's the secret, baby! If you keep positive energy flowing in your life, you will attract positive situations and better outcomes. But this can only be done by developing mental toughness, understanding your purpose and becoming in tuned with yourself. You must be confident if you're going to survive all that I have discussed in this chapter. So, how does someone who has experienced so much early childhood trauma/drama develop confidence? Well, I can tell you that developing mental toughness has built my confidence, and as I continued to strengthen my mental toughness, my confidence also increased.

For me, I have always worked to strengthen myself through reading self-help materials and through my discovery of meditation.

Mediation is the art of becoming aware of your breathing, your energy, and being present in the moment. Practicing various forms of meditation helps focus your mind and submerge your mental state into the present moment.

When I'm fully immersed in the present moment, I end any thoughts of what happened in my past and avoid over thinking and projecting into the future. Instead, I only focus on what needs to happen in this now moment. Bringing my thoughts under control and developing the ability to still my mind and meditate builds my confidence. I maintained my meditation practice throughout my football career and have since made it part of my lifestyle. I maintain this practice because doing so hasn't failed me yet.

But, I must tell you that none of the techniques I have shared will work for you unless you have a big-picture understanding of your destination. For as long as I can remember, personal success was my destination. Success looks different for each person. For me, attaining Life Wealth is the definition of success. From a big-picture perspective, I'm able to view my life in chapters.

First came my departure from torture and abuse. Then, I went on to build skills that would lead to mental, spiritual, financial, and physical health. Finally, I used those skills and techniques to drive me towards Life Wealth and ultimate success. Big picture thinking is needed to understand your destination. By having a big-picture view of life, small detours aren't as deflating.

So, every step of the way, I visualize and maintain my focus on the big picture.

In January of every year, I create goals in each of the Life Wealth pillars that I will focus on for that year. The goals are intentionally selected to bring me closer to complete balance. As an example, the year I wrote this book, I created four goals; complete my book, receive a promotion at work, work out at least three days a week and eat healthier, and improve my family relationships. That's how I strategize for the win in my life on every level of the playing field.

When I was playing football, it was important to understand the coach's game plan and what my role was in that plan. In life, it is even more critical for me to visualize where I want to take my life from a big-picture perspective because I am the coach. It's my job to envision and plan for each phase of my life, from college to retirement. I also try to be inclusive of the four pillars of Life Wealth when viewing the overall game plan. So I have to think about how I will continue to grow from a spiritual, mental, physical, and financial perspective.

In football and in life, achieving success required me to make key connections and network with people who might support my strategy. I understood early on that I cannot adequately convey to my network where I need their help unless I know my plan and can communicate it. Once I know what I need, I can better access the resources my network offers, and plug them in where needed. I pay attention to building and nurturing relationships that would benefit my journey to success that creates mutual benefits for both parties.

As stated several times already, the strategy and journey to success will be long and require hard work, but with persistence, success is inevitable. But you must be able to fine-tune your approach for the stage of the plan you're executing at the moment.

For instance, In high school, playing football required practicing twice a day in the preseason, weight training, play book study, and the upkeep of your academic work. That workload becomes even harder in college, where the responsibilities of student life begin to resemble a full-time job.

During spring semesters in college, I had to attend 6 am workouts and then go to class immediately following. I returned to the gym for weight training, and then I went to study hall before my next class. It would have been easy to become discouraged and give up, but remember, it is at these points in life when you most need a strong mentality and the discipline to be persistent in your actions. So I kept growing!

Staying positive doesn't guarantee you a quality performance. Paying attention to your output does! If my performance wasn't excellent, I would have lost my position to someone who could deliver consistently. As I moved to higher levels of play, the need to deliver quality results consistently became even more necessary. This concept also holds true for my family life and my career. Discipline, hard work, and a good strategy allows me to maintain the quality of my performance.

Naturally, working hard goes without saying for any driven person. Developing a good work ethic is a positive characteristic that came out of my abusive childhood. I have always embraced my ability to work harder than most of my peers, and this is still mostly true to this day. In my opinion and experience, hard work is almost synonymous with rural farm life, and I knew something about both.

At a very young age, I was expected to perform at the same level and output the same quality of work as a grown-up. Because of my drive, I always wanted to perform well, so it became part of my personality, and it carried over into adolescence and adulthood-- whether it was about football or life.

One of my favorite quotes by Tim Notke is, "hard work beats talent if talent doesn't work hard." So, I made sure that I had talent and worked hard. I am confident in my talent, and I assure you that you will not outwork me!

Now, I know that the last statement may make me sound a bit cocky, but it was intentionally stated this way to showcase my level of confidence. But, maintaining humility is a far more important attribute to develop than confidence. Humility, by definition, is having or showing a modest estimate of one's importance. From my vantage point, this doesn't mean a lack of confidence.

Confidence and humility are challenging traits to develop when you feel life has been whipping your ass from the time you were born. I had a bad childhood, and because of it, I understand how bad life can be for others. I also understand life can be a lot worse. So, when I achieve success based on my strategy (life plan), I work hard not to take that success for granted. I embrace the success of the moment while simultaneously realizing others have achieved the same and more, which helps keep me humble. As Americans, we often inflate our accomplishments as a means of self-motivation without realizing that others have achieved the same level of success. You must find better, and more creative ways to motivate yourself. Never rest on the accomplishments of yesterday; always assess yourself appropriately! For me, it just means I don't embellish my accomplishments to unrealistic heights to feel like I'm performing better than I truly am.

In sports, there are always bigger, faster, and more athletic people around you. In life, you can also assume there are always going to be people who are better educated, more charming, or better connected than you are, but that certainly doesn't diminish the value you bring, and it does not mean you are worthless.

As an example, when I left high school, I was extremely physically fit and at the height of my athleticism. I was six feet tall and around one hundred and eighty-five pounds. My body's fat percentage was about five percent, which means you could see my muscle strands. I ran the forty-yard dash in 4.4 seconds. That's pretty damn fast!

My confidence in my ability to perform was somewhat inflated, but I didn't know that until I went to college, where I met Jason Davis.

Jason was built much like me and presented with the same warrior heart. However, Jason was five inches taller, and he ran the forty in 4.35 seconds! So, there I was, thinking I was the man and this dude was, in every physical aspect, a better specimen for the game of football. Luckily we played different positions, and we both were very good at what we did for the team.

Meeting another man who was just as talented and driven to be the best football player on the field taught me a valuable lesson about humility. Having him to compare myself to made me have to focus on optimizing my skills and talents without the need to embellish them.

Thankfully, that didn't cause me to shy away from the desire to be my best and to play a good game of football every time I hit the field. His showing up caused me to apply even more effort to becoming the best player I could be.

Conversely, my stepfather's negative response to my desire to play football and acquire a scholarship didn't shut down my aspirations. His mocking tone and disbelief only made me more determined to push through and achieve that life goal.

Along the way, I learned valuable lessons and realized some additional skills I could apply to my life. Although these lessons were obtained through trial and error, they have proven to be what I needed to accomplish my life goals.

That's Life

~

PART-FOUR

Life Wealth

As a child, there were so many times where I wondered what life was trying to do to me. Why was it necessary for me to struggle so much? I tried very hard to get ahead, but I always seemed to run into a brick wall that stopped me dead in my tracks. I was tired of struggling and being poor.

A staggering number of Black families go through the same thought process every day. Our minds are always wondering why we never get the breakthrough our pastor preaches about every Sunday. We wonder if there's some secret about life we don't know that everyone else does.

The truth is, there is no secret. However, I believe it's necessary to ask questions about poverty. Perhaps some people would say insufficient finances is poverty. Others would say family and love is wealth, so the lack of family and love is the same as being poor. I believe the concept of wealth is multi-faceted and complex, but so is the construct of poverty. There is a balance to be aware of to avoid tipping the scale into poverty and an empty life.

I believe there are four distinct qualities needed to obtain wealth in life. Let's call the existence and balance of these four attributes, "Life Wealth." Lacking these four qualities will move a person's current state closer to being "Life Poor."

Spiritual Health

Spiritual health (Spirit) allows you to be in touch with and work toward a greater purpose, to be at peace with yourself, and to become fully present and understand the connection between you and everything in your life. The characteristic of spiritual health has the most significant positive influence on the other aspects of your life. Therefore, spirituality should be focused on, obtained, and increased first. Many people go to church to achieve spiritual health; others meditate to find peace. Paying attention to your breathing is also a way of becoming acquainted with your true self and your spirituality. No matter the method you use to improve your spiritual health, focus on becoming aware of your current state, which is the start of becoming "Life Wealthy."

Mental Health

Your mental health (Soul) is closely tied to your spiritual state. All my life, I've heard the saying, "education is key." However, when considering "Life Wealth," education is only a means of obtaining good mental health. Many people struggle to control their thoughts, especially if they are linked to a traumatic event. Those thoughts may lead to more traumatic events and take you further away from developing positive mental health. Your negative thoughts must be categorized and filed away in your mental cabinet like any other tool or piece of information. You can access those thoughts when you need them. Controlling your thoughts will bring you closer to developing greater mental health, which will move you closer to "life wealth."

Physical Health

Physical health (Body) is what most people associate with being healthy. The body is very similar to any machine. Performing routine maintenance on the body systems supports longevity. Rest and regular exercise should be considered routine maintenance. There is nothing innovative about the above statements. However, 47.9% of non-Hispanic Blacks are obese in America. Black males and females are almost twice as likely to have diabetes than their white and Asian counterparts. This information is well known in Black communities, but the numbers continue to grow. Preservation of the body supports the maintenance of the mind and promotes spiritual growth.

These first three attributes of Life Wealth are all closely related and inter-dependent on each other. For instance, paying attention to your thoughts (mental health) often leads to developing stronger faith (spiritual health) in your ability to control your thoughts through meditation and prayer. And as you control your thoughts, you will also pay closer attention to your body (physical health). Your mental and physical health increases as you increase in spiritual health. Which is why we started with building spiritual health; it is the foundation of your success.

Financial Health

The final quality that constitutes Life Wealth is financial health (Material Possessions). Lack of finances negatively impacts Black Americans inter-generationally more than any other ethnicity in America. Maintaining your financial health is as important as building your spiritual health but in a different way. Lack of finances causes most people to lose focus on all the other attributes of wealth. It is common to see a person neglect their spiritual, mental, and physical health to increase financial wealth. Sometimes, it is necessary to ignore one quality to improve another. However, complete neglect undermines a person's overall Life Wealth. Black Americans are especially susceptible to the adverse effects of not having a strong financial background. We have been conditioned to believe that a lack of financial stability means you are not worthy or smart. And, because Black Americans possess such a small percentage of America's financial wealth, we often feel inferior. In this case, perception is not reality. Remember, we have been made to believe that monetary gains equal happiness, but I assure you that isn't always the case. Financial stability is a tool that allows you to enjoy life better; it doesn't mean life cannot be enjoyable in its absence. The brain must be re-trained to only think in ways that move you closer to Life Wealth.

Finding Balance While Building Life Wealth

Neglecting any of the four attributes of Life Wealth moves you into the direction of being Life Poor. Not having a strong spiritual foundation and practice diminishes your Life Wealth and potentially impacts the other three areas dramatically. So, it's important to maintain healthy spiritual practices, to exercise your mind and body, and only engage in activities that ensure your financial stability so you can enjoy life.

Because the concept of developing Life Wealth is somewhat complicated, I would like to discuss, in more detail, the attributes of wealth building and the risk one takes by remaining poor. Specifically, I would like to explore the interpretation of wealth vs. poverty as it relates to the Black Community in America.

Do Black Americans identify with the construct of poverty because of the lack of monetary wealth and possessions, or is there an understanding that wealth is a combination of spiritual, mental, physical, and financial fitness? How does the lack of support in the Black community impact our overall "Life Wealth"? Is the perception of poverty different for each ethnic group? How can a person change his/her condition from one of scarcity to one of wealth?

If I reflect on my childhood when I consider those questions, I must observe the mentality of my community at the time and reflect on the progression of my thought process as I grew over the years. What changed about how I thought? What remained the same? What should have changed? The expected outcome of such an exploration should expose unhealthy thinking patterns and behaviors to clarify how we can better define Life Wealth.

There is a social hierarchy in America, and it's based on things like education, income, where we live, social status, class, caste, etc. Well, would it surprise you to learn that there are several more levels to the social hierarchy among poor people in America? Oh, yes, sir!

And, like any other hierarchy in America, poor people are arranged by rank--and dead broke families are at the bottom of that hierarchy, as you might imagine.

The upper layer amongst the poor live paycheck to paycheck. They're not exactly broke, but they would surely crumble if an emergency occurs, like getting a flat tire or a broken arm. These families are at the highest level among the "broke folk" even though, in the eyes of American society overall, they would be considered "poor."

Despite the odds, my mother always had a job even if it didn't pay very much. She provided for her children as best she could. However, my earliest childhood memories are of being broke, having an incomplete and broken family structure, and, from my perspective, absolutely no love to give one another. We were *completely* broke because we were "Life Poor," and we would suffer for years with spiritual, mental, and financial deficiencies well into our adult lives because of it.

My mother was a young, single mother without a high school diploma, so it was hard for her to find work that could support raising two growing boys. My small hometown was rural, racist, and economically challenged. So the combination of not having an education and living in a town where jobs were scarce made it difficult for my mother to improve her finances. So we were, naturally, at the lowest level of the definition of poverty.

My mother, Tommy, and I lived with my grandmother for the first years of my life. Life was difficult because, by the time she was 17, she had two children. Her Life Wealth had not even started to develop at that point, but it would be even more challenging to acquire while simultaneously raising two active boys. Dropping out of school in the ninth grade ensured that there would be many mental, emotional, and financial barriers she would have to overcome while on her Life Wealth journey.

My mother always seemed to be on edge and easily angered. This anger often would lead to her yelling and distributing arbitrary spankings. Sometimes, her rage would lead to sessions of full-on abuse. Honestly, who could blame her? Having two active, rambunctious boys, no education, and a dead-end job certainly made her behavior and disposition justified. And my grandmother's constant ridicule of her situation most certainly pushed her stress levels even higher.

As an adult, I can understand that my mother was stressed, depressed, and beaten down. She felt like life's punching bag. Mentally, she would fight herself just to get motivated to go to work every morning. Then she would fight her way home and struggle to find food and make our dinner before she could finally go to sleep; then wake up to do it all again. I now understand that she was freaking exhausted! As she continued this fight, she became less motivated to be a good mother. Her frustrations grew, and her mental strength diminished tremendously.

My brother and I would suffer physical, mental, and emotional abuse as a result of her frustrations and because she didn't know how to handle the stress. She was already working from a deficit based on the lack of education. Considering strategies that would increase her Life Wealth never had the chance to balance. The world didn't care about her deficits or what she didn't receive from her mother. They viewed her as an unfit mother, regardless of her shortcomings as she entered the role of mothering! Considering how many Black Americans enter "The Real World" from a place of lack, any time one of us wins, there should be a celebration.

During my early childhood, there were many violations of the Life Wealth code. The Life Wealth disparity created my mother's financial condition and her inability to acquire sufficient finances to care for two kids. Based on her early financial struggles, my mother incurred insurmountable levels of mental strain.

If you analyze my mother's adolescent life, you would realize that having my brother and me so early in life impacted my mother's ability to amass Life Wealth. Becoming a mother of two children by the age of 17 with no male support created obstacles that were difficult to accept and, much less, overcome.

Let's go a step further. Tommy is three years older than me, which means my mother was 14 years old when she gave birth to him. Overcoming adversity and becoming a responsible mother at 14 is overwhelming, at best. Finding out that you will have two kids before your 18th birthday without an income is an experience that can create deep trauma and emotional shock. As an adult, I can see that my mother was traumatized long before she traumatized my brother and me.

My mother's mental health was compromised based on her lack of education. The ability to problem solve a situation this dire isn't fully developed by the age of 14, so having to face these problems alone caused her further emotional trauma. Her mental state shifted and her Life Wealth balance became unstable.

Suffering abuse as a child isn't uncommon in Black communities. Many Black households are frustrated, stressed, and depressed. The root cause is an imbalance in their Life Wealth-- stemming from a lack of financial stability, insufficient mental strength, or other variables that have nothing to do with the child, they are just born into these situations.

My mother turned to the church as a means of making her life better. Seeking spiritual guidance and direction was the best way she could think of to maintain her sanity while going through this unimaginable hell. Yes, I'm saying she went through hell because that must have been what it was like to deal with the torment of living the same stressful day, over and over again, for years.

When I was seven years old, my mother married Charles. I believe she thought it would allow her to overcome the impossible odds stacked against her. And though I didn't like or trust him, my desire to have a father figure in my life minimized my uneasiness. Besides, with a father figure in the house, we would either move further up the "poor" social ladder or out of the poverty class completely. I imagined that my mother wouldn't have to carry the painfully heavy load of raising us boys alone. She would have the kind of help that would allow us to live better. So, I was pleased and excited to have this mysterious fellow visiting my mother—at first. I began to see his presence as the end of being poor.

Even though I was too young to express my anticipation in those terms, I was excited to have a man around, and I dreamed of what it might be like not to struggle so much. On some level, I was aware of the social status of my family and, damn it, I was already sick of it!

Shortly after my mother married Charles, my family moved from the economically challenged town of Pelham to the even more income deficient countryside of Thomasville. But the idea of moving into a new home was exciting and fun. My brother and I couldn't sit still due to our excitement and anticipation. However, we were quickly disappointed when we discovered that we were moving into a home with Charles' mother and younger brother. Now, six of us occupied a tiny 3-bedroom trailer-style home that sat in the middle of a half-acre country yard.

At the back right corner of the yard was an enormous labyrinth, constructed strictly for the amusement of Charles' rabbit collection. It's incredible to reflect on a family of 6 living in a thousand-square-foot, dilapidated home, replete with gaping holes in the floor of the kitchen and bathroom. Protection from the southern Georgia elements was nonexistent, so winter winds cut through our paper-thin walls like a hot knife through butter. During this transition, it was apparent to me (the seven-year-old) that my family had moved further down in social status—we were now "dirt poor."

My siblings and I wore the same torn and dirt-stained clothes for years, regardless of them being 2 or 3 sizes too small. The other "broke families" that lived near us referred to my family as "the poor ones down the street." They knew my family's living condition was even worse than theirs. So, even though my mother married this dude to escape poverty, we were now officially at the bottom of the hierarchy—which was even worse than where we began.

I was teased and bullied by the kids in the area because they perceived that I was beneath them from a financial perspective. However, growing up in a shack and being more impoverished than other kids was just the surface truth of who I was. But poverty thinking was ingrained in my family's DNA and seemed to be present in all of my ancestors' lives.

To the average American, poverty is the inability to accumulate material possessions. Big homes, expensive cars, fancy jewelry, nice clothes, and vacation properties seem to signify wealth. Poverty is the opposite of wealth, and based on typical American standards.

I grew up without some of the things that make life enjoyable. Despite growing up in church and practically living in the pews, I was still spiritually depleted. In my opinion, the lack of spirituality, self-esteem, motivation, and financial stability is the definition of poverty.

My affliction as a child was that I pondered life concepts that many adults around me seemed to ignore. For example, my expectation of attending church was that we would grow in love through a spiritual relationship with God. Some churchgoers grow their spiritual relationship with God as expected, but because of the people in my life and my surroundings, I struggled to witness real love.

For as long as I can remember, my emotions and thoughts were mixed and somewhat complicated for a child my age. Sure, I smiled and seemingly enjoyed playing with my peers, but my thoughts always turned inwardly, and I wondered why I couldn't find the same joy they seemed to have. Why couldn't I be content with my environment like everyone else around me seemed to be?

Those kids did not understand they were in poverty, and therefore, they didn't care. But my emotional maturity caused my eyes to see things they didn't, and that made me an unfit playmate because I was often depressed by the things I knew about life. As I grew older, my perspective began to change, and I focused on prosperity.

Prosperity has become a familiar buzz word these days and is a popular sermon topic in many churches. I would like to understand what makes a person prosperous. Is it Money? Is it material wealth like boats, luxury cars, beautiful clothing, designer purses?

Prosperity is different from my perspective. Your "being" is composed of your spirit, mind, and body. Neglect of any aspect of your being moves you away from prosperity. So, the opposite of prosperity is poverty. Taking care of the four Life Wealth qualities increases your prosperity. That is where my focus is now and where my focus will be until I can "be" no more.

Points to Remember: Spiritual Health

Your relationship with everything around you is part of spirituality. Cultivating compassion for everyone and everything around you grows your capacity for experiencing love and allows you to participate in the essential act of forgiveness. Being unselfish brings joy to yourself and others, and greatly improves your spiritual health. Focusing on developing all of these attributes at once is a lot of work. But throughout your lifetime, you should be working to improve them all.

Points to Remember: Mental Health

Addressing and coping with poor mental health is difficult in today's world. Remember, mental health relates to a person's condition regarding their psychological and emotional well-being. To accurately assess your mental wellness, find a mental health professional to talk with about your issues and any traumatic experiences you have had to determine whether you would benefit from ongoing counselling. Also, mediation is a huge help if your conflict involves others.

Points to Remember: Physical Health

Physical health can be defined as an essential part of the overall health of an individual and includes everything from physical fitness to your overall well-being. Improving this quality can be easier to address because you can see the results of your work more easily. Working out, becoming active and paying attention to what you are putting into your body are easy things to do that can lead you to some rather positive outcomes.

Points to Remember: Financial Health

Finally, financial health is a term used to describe the state of your financial situation. There are many dimensions to financial health, including the amount of savings you have, how much you are setting aside for retirement, and how much income you are spending on legitimate expenses and how much disposable income you have. Get a financial coach or advisor to help you in this area if you don't have one already. Keep in mind that gaining more financial wealth doesn't guarantee you will be happier.

My Personal LIFE WEALTH Balance

Based on my viewpoint about life and wealth, I began to recognize that I needed to focus on building my Life Wealth balance, too. I needed to make tremendous improvements in my spiritual and mental attributes. I realized I had to dive deeper into my spiritual and mental health by addressing all the abuse from my past that compromised my overall health.

Constant thoughts that made me confused, sad, and anxious are the side effects of my abuse. As a result, I went on autopilot in my life and mentally withdrew from my surroundings. My teachers would always comment on how smart I was but said I didn't focus enough. When I wasn't thinking deeply about my future, I was always thinking about the past and what happened to me as a child. I was in a constant loop of ruminating thoughts, so my level of confusion increased-- which further clouded my thoughts.

I was a sophomore in college when I realized I needed to develop a method of coping with these thoughts and feelings. During my college days, I was very lonely; I was a thousand miles away from Auntie and the rest of my family, and I had no friends. I played football, which provided a physical outlet for painful emotions, but I couldn't control my feelings completely. One day when I was a freshman, I lost control of myself during a game because I had a chip on my shoulder, and I was emotionally explosive.

We were playing our conference rivals, so it was a big game. James Dunkin was the starting strong safety, and I was playing cornerback on his side. My receiver would run straight and block the strong safety, which is called a "crack on the safety." This block was dangerous because James never saw it coming. So, to protect the strong safety, the cornerback is supposed to yell "crack, crack" as an alert. However, because I was young and naïve, I didn't realize that. The first time this happened to James, he was knocked to the ground.

He came to me after the play and said, "call the crack baby, you gonna get me hurt, Lil Man."

Well, a couple of plays later, the same thing happened. The receiver v-lined towards James and cleaned his clock. At that point, I had an "oh shit" moment. I didn't catch it fast enough because the pace of the game was much faster than it was in High School, and my mind wasn't able to keep up.

James, now with a little more irritation in his body language, said to me, "Dawg…you gotta let me know the dude is coming, man. That shit hurts. Come on, baby, let's get it!"

In retrospect, he was able to control his emotions very well despite being completely killed by the receiver. I felt terrible at that point because I sincerely wanted to do the right thing. But because I was so thrilled to be playing as a freshman, the mixed emotions of excitement and fear that came with the experience overcame me, and I just plain forgot to send the alert again. James was taken off his feet by the same receiver. This time the receiver laughed at James, literally adding insult to injury.

James, wearing a look of frustration, came directly to me and yelled in my face this time: "Dawg…call…the fucking…crack!"

This is where I lost it. James had shown extreme control over his emotions twice to teach me how to play the game. Yet, I couldn't control mine once to show appreciation.

So, with my ego in hand, I responded in a louder voice, "fuck you, man!"

A hush seemed to fall over the entire crowd of forty thousand fans as if they heard every word. I felt horrible afterward. The coaching staff was totally disgusted and displeased with my lack of control, and in an instant, I lost a would-be mentor.

It was a prime example of what can happen when your emotions are controlling because you haven't worked through your issues. I was forced to face the fact that I needed help dealing with my emotions, and I couldn't operate the same way anymore.

I understood that my past was negatively impacting my career and my social standing among my peers. Nobody wants to hang out with Angry Man all the time! Coming to terms with those emotions was important. So, I joined a local church to begin working on my spirituality. I became more centered and self-aware through meditation and reading self-help books.

Meditation and breathing exercises helped me remain calm and diminished my "out of control thoughts and emotions." It was challenging at first, but now I can see how it changed me for the better.

Because of those breathing techniques, my thoughts became less of a problem. The confusion that once plagued my mind began to clear up. My self-confidence and motivation grew as I grounded myself in the art of meditation. As I cleared away my confusion and calmed my emotions, I improved my ability to visualize my true spirit. And people around me began to take notice of how different I was; people started liking me more because I started loving myself! The benefits of meditation are immeasurable, and the feeling it gives me is fantastic!

Immediately after I meditate, I try to limit the amount of information I take in that doesn't originate from within by avoiding things like the news; I hold off on having conversations that aren't necessary, and I definitely stay away from social media whenever possible and for as long as possible. Taking in too much information can cause your mental and emotional state to be weakened, so it's important to periodically unplug from friends and family to protect your thoughts and emotions. Detaching myself from all information is not necessary, but protecting myself from overexposure to outside stimulation improves the quality of my thoughts and emotions; it has made a noticeable difference in how I interact with people around me.

Now that I meditate, I'm able to scan my body and read the quality of my energy and my body's overall health. When I eliminated a lot of the external noise from my daily routine, I could hear and better understand my true self. Meditation is the way I separate myself from the madness in the world around me.

There are three key elements I use to ensure I receive the maximum benefit of meditating, and I will share them with you in the hopes that you will allow meditation to transform your life, too.

Controlling my breathing is the first and most essential part of meditation. When practicing yoga and meditation, we know that breath is life. It is energy. Therefore, I practice observing my breath at various times, especially when I am dealing with challenging thoughts and emotions. When I experience sadness, I noticed that my breathing takes on a slow, deep, and heavy pace. When I'm angry, my breathing is rapid and shallow. Breath awareness allows me to return to a relaxed, normal breathing pace--regardless of the situation. It's easier said than done, which is why I practice my breathing exercises daily.

The second key element of meditation is becoming aware of the thoughts that occupy my mind. It is normal to have random thoughts come and go through my mind, but when they do, I turn my attention to controlling my breathing and allow the thoughts to come and go. I know I can't stop breathing, and I can't stop my thoughts from coming, but I can visualize them like waves in the ocean and myself as a surfer, waiting on the perfect wave to jump. As I meditate, I let thoughts pass without growing attached to them. I let them come--and go, which usually takes no more than five seconds now that I've been practicing for some time. When I notice a thought that is problematic or profound, I still do nothing with the thought during meditation because if the thought is profound enough, I won't forget it, and I can write it down later. My ability to allow thoughts to flow has become more noticeable. And, I've become more proficient at controlling my thoughts during times when I am not meditating. As a result, the thoughts I pay attention to are of a much higher quality.

The third and last key element of my meditation is observing the energy within my body. Once I can control my breathing and thoughts, I have room to pay attention to my energy. If I identify energy that isn't helpful or positive, I can create techniques to change my mood. It is inevitable to feel sadness, anger, excitement, and a plethora of other emotions throughout life. Breathing and thought management have helped me have some level of control over how those emotions impact my life. Monitoring your energy and emotions is the hardest of the three key elements to master, but if practiced and developed, the impact it will have on your life is amazing.

Sadness was a common emotion I experienced due to my past. And the more I thought about what happened to me and why, the deeper the sadness within me grew. I began to notice that the more sadness I had, the more frequently I thought about things that caused sadness! It can be a never-ending cycle of negative thoughts and emotions.

Meditation helps me manage my past and future thoughts by making me focus on the present and nothing more This helped me avoid sad and anxious emotions. As a result, my mental health has improved dramatically. But meditation isn't the only tool in the box that has helped me grow my Life Wealth. It wasn't until recently that I discovered how beneficial talking with someone about my life could be.

For over thirty years, I did not share my thoughts and past experiences, not even with people close to me. I just kept them in a dusty box stored in the back of my head. Also, inside that dusty box are suppressed emotions, which also carried negative energy with them. Discussing my experiences with a counselor helped me release those negative emotions and transform the energy surrounding them. It created a huge shift in my life because, until that point, I was successful at avoiding and suppressing my feelings.

For a long time, I could only view my past from my vantage point. One day, it dawned on me that if I couldn't see beyond my own ideas about life, I would never be healed of my past because I would stay within my personal interpretations of every situation. And I was at risk of making so many more incorrect interpretations because I assumed everyone thought the same way I did.

Talking with a counselor, friends, and family members opened me up to other ideas, viewpoints, and thoughts. Now, and whenever possible, I seek input from people around me to ensure I am taking a holistic approach to life. Talking to others helps me process those experiences in a better way.

Consulting a therapist allowed me to discover that I have issues around trust and loyalty. I had been beaten and battered by the people who should have loved me, so I began to believe that if they were capable of such atrocities, I could not trust anyone to care for me.

I have seen the same behavior in my brother and other male friends. We shut down our emotions and revert to toughness. As black males, we suffer from depression and sadness like everyone else, but we tend to shut down our feelings to avoid looking soft. But if you find someone in whom you can confide and tell your truth, you might notice a considerable difference in your ability to overcome your emotional issues.

If someone confides in you, it is crucial not to judge them for the things they share. I don't take the role of being a confidant lightly because they have to be able to trust that I have their best interest in mind when they share or seek advice from me.

There are three key aspects I consider when I decide to talk with someone and get their interpretation of my situation.

First, the person I discuss my hurtful life experiences with must be trust-worthy. I've been through hell already, so I'm not looking for anyone to give me a second tour of the place! They must be able to make me feel comfortable and safe by protecting my truth. Family and friends I've shared with have proven that I can trust them over time. An easier way to ensure the necessary trust is in place is by utilizing a licensed counselor. Counselors are governed by client confidentiality agreements, so they aren't allowed to share anything you've discussed. Finding a professional counselor may be a better route to take if you have difficulty trusting until you become better able and more willing to let other people into your world.

Secondly, I always ensure my confidants are spiritually mature and have the mental capacity to hear about my traumatic experiences. I have many friends, but not all of them can handle hearing about some of the things that have transpired in my life. The last thing I need is someone going into a state of depression based on the story of my life. That would create more sorrow in me.

Lastly, ensuring the person is non-judgmental is very important. It is crucial to confide in someone with a non-judgmental ear if you're planning on using informal talk therapy with a friend or loved one..

Through routine discussions about my most traumatic experiences, I was able to identify the emotional triggers associated with them. Now I know that my triggers are based on the abuse and neglect I received from my mother.

As an example, because I was physically abused as a child, I'm hyper-protective of anyone being harmed. If I see aggression against someone incapable of defending themselves, I immediately move in to protect them. Good or bad, that's one of my triggers. Once I identified the trigger, I could better manage the outcome by understanding the specific situation that caused my reaction. I realized that my responses were closely related to my ego. I often think, "how dare you abuse this person?" and I know that it's because I was abused. Knowing that's the root of my response allows me to talk myself out of responding angrily.

But You Can

PART-FIVE

Pay Attention To Others

Because of the trauma associated with my abuse, I'm very observant of the energy of people around me. I had to spend a lot of time reading people and picking up on small things about them for my safety. At a very early age, I was able to tell when someone had deep-seated emotional issues--even if other people didn't notice. And now, I can better read people, which allows me to adjust my behavior to make them feel comfortable and improve the relationship we are building. I developed a deep desire to pay close attention to what people need so I could help them heal.

To heal myself, I read many self-help books because I wanted, more than anything, to understand how to manage the thoughts and emotions that seemed to run wild in my mind like cowboys in an old western movie. I kept observing myself, and eventually, I noticed similar characteristics in other people around me. They couldn't stay focused, and they were emotionally explosive, just like me. And because I understood what they were going through, I discovered that I could ease their stress. After a while, I developed the ability to motivate and push people to operate at their highest potential without causing them additional stress. I was getting positive results, too. People thanked me for helping them grow and become better human beings by listening and by paying attention to their needs. But I may not have developed this capability without my past experiences.

Set Yourself Free - Independence

Having to rely upon my own efforts in order to survive gave me the kind of independence that cannot be taught. Even now, I am independent to a fault; and as a result, I really struggle when I have to rely on other people.

I understand the need to have someone I can rely on to make things easier, and I accept that kind of support when it's available. But rest assured, I always believe I can get things done with or without the help of others. That is the epitome of independence, in my opinion, and I embrace it fully! My independent spirit is a very positive result of my dark past. If it were not for that very independence, my chances of failure in life would have been much, much higher.

The Survivor's Innovation

Developing innovative thinking skills helped me solve life problems--problems like how I was going to earn money or find food and shelter. It was common for me to go some nights, even full days, without a bite to eat. Thinking outside the box was a necessary means of survival, and that skill has stuck with me.

The typical child has a stable home where parents are responsible for all of the decisions concerning their lives, and they plan for and address whatever problems arise with those children. But, I lacked parental guidance, so all of the problem-solving tasks were left to me. Luckily, I was the kind of person who was determined not to let the lack of support stand in the way of my goals. I became determined to win in spite of the obstacles before me.

Just before the start of my first year playing football, I faced an obstacle I was sure I couldn't overcome, but with a little bit of creative problem solving, I did!

I had no money to pay for equipment, the physical, or my cleats. And I didn't exactly have a ride to and from practice. I had to solve the problem. Football was my only means of receiving a college education, so I knew I had to perform at a very high level if I was going to receive a scholarship.

I immediately began to think about how to use my resources to create an innovative solution for this problem. I began to use my barbering skills to earn money for the fees and the equipment, and I arranged my transportation to practice by providing an older teammate that had his own car with free weekly haircuts. It wasn't an impossible problem to solve; I just had to think outside the box.

I Hate Hate

Turning all the negative experiences into positive ones became relatively easy when I connected them to professional skills or messages that align with self-help. But the most challenging thing I had to face was addressing my abuse and the hate my family seemed to have for me. How could I turn that into a positive?

Everyone on this planet has some kind of mental hang up. Some people will admit they have a psychological issue. Others choose not to accept their mental issues. Unfortunately, there are those people who inflict abuse on people around them--physically, emotionally, and sexually. I was the victim of a couple of those persons.

As a result of their hatred, I became consumed by that same hate until it permeated every aspect of my life, like maggots feasting on rotting flesh.

Here are two interesting points I discovered about hatred. One, the people who caused me pain and trauma must've hated themselves, too, if they could perform such atrocious acts. The other is that they transferred these feelings to me and caused me to hate myself because of the pain and trauma I experienced at their hands. I started out hating them for what they did, but hating them made me hate myself!

It took over twenty years of work, meditation, and positive re-enforcement to get rid of the hate.

But I can't lie and say the hate is gone entirely—it just took a different, healthier form. I sometimes smell its foul odor in the presence of people with a hateful spirit. I now have hate radar. It goes off when I sense hateful energy, and it immediately sends me into combat mode! That's is the negative side of being abused as a child--the hate always resides in you. I really don't like people with hateful energy, and I have taught myself to tune it out and remove myself from its presence.

So now, I am pro-love! I love everything about love, and I actively search for the love that lives in everyone, especially myself. My energy level gets stronger when I sense love in others. And now, I also have love radar, and I use it to generate more love in myself and in others. I have a passion for love because it was sorely missing from my early life. I honor my journey from hate to the ultimate destination in life--which is love. So, yeah, I absolutely love…love!

The Slave Mentality--Just Let it Go, Man!!

I now believe my mom had mental immaturity, which resulted in her slave mentality. I base this belief on the way she cared for and handled her children. The cruel and unusual punishments she inflicted on us resembled those of a brutal and heartless slave master. When I was younger, I was incapable of seeing the relationship between her punishments and the things Black people endured during slavery because my brain had not matured enough to draw those parallels. I didn't have the capacity to think critically about this as a child; I only knew that her actions seemed awfully harsh, especially coming from someone who was supposed to protect me from the harshness of the world.

My mom could not admit that the way she expressed her anger was an issue because of her personal history and the environment in which she grew. The mindset and morality one uses when raising children is passed down from generation to generation in any family. Many of my relatives were raised in the same type of abusive environment as I was. It was commonplace to hear that if your child spoke out of turn, you should whoop their ass to guarantee they wouldn't do it again. If your child was running around the house and wouldn't sit down, just grab a switch from a tree and tap those legs—I'll bet they won't get up anymore! Such proclamations were commonplace and often practiced in my family. It's what they knew.

It was also how the slave master maintained control of his human chattel.

My mother couldn't identify slave-like mentality because it was very normal to her. Neglectful and violent behavior was just the way everyone in the family behaved, so she didn't view it as abnormal or problematic. She was blind to her own pain, so she couldn't see how her behavior negatively impacted her children.

As an ethnic group, African Americans have to develop an ability to identify these flaws in our mentality. The concept of slave mentality goes beyond the way we discipline children and impacts every aspect of how we live our lives. Therefore, as a group, we should focus on attaining "Life Wealth" to begin ridding ourselves of this harmful way of thinking.

Because my mom was incapable of seeing her flaws, she couldn't accept that she had a poor mindset. She never showed remorse for her actions, not even when confronted about tying my brother to the bedposts and beating him bloody, or slapping me with all her might-- enough to cause my eye to bleed! Never did she show any remorse or sympathy for those she hurt.

Now, I get that my older brother was entirely out of line for taking that soda and opening it in the store despite not having the money to pay. Even at that age, I knew that was wrong. However, the punishment that followed was not warranted. My mother never acknowledged that her punishments were cruel and unusual. To me, this very closely resembles the punishment historically administered by the slave master for minimal infractions. Her behavior didn't change because the mentality that spawned it was never identified as problematic.

My mom had an extremely difficult time controlling her emotions. Anything could set her off (and often would) because she lacked the mental and spiritual maturity to manage her feelings. So, my brother and I suffered tremendously at her hands.

The inability to control her emotions was not entirely her fault. She learned, from generations before her, how to react in the manner she did. Highly volatile reactions are commonplace in my family tree. I have no data to prove this out, but it seems we de-humanized ourselves and one another at an alarming rate. By reacting in a volatile manner and passing the behavior down through generations, we continue the slave master's practices of de-humanizing us--which causes the mentality to persist well after slavery was outlawed. My mother was slow to break the chains of her mental enslavement. It wasn't until after I was an adult that she realized her flawed perspective.

The reason why this slave mentality has lasted so long is due to a lack of self-love. As a society, we have yet to reverse the perspective that the descendants of slaves are not human. There are, obviously, individuals and even groups who do not operate under this notion. However, the majority of American society continues to hold this idea, and they behave as if it is an irrefutable fact.

Slaves were taught to hate everything about themselves, and the slave master went to great lengths to create a psyche of inferiority. The abuse of our children, women, and one another as Black men proves that we suffer from a lack of self-love.

The perpetuation of this slave mentality continues when families continue to use unhealthy methods to control their children. It is untrue that if you are not beating your kids, you are spoiling them. This concept is presented in the Bible, so it's "the law" in many poor Black families--thus, the mentality perpetuates. I believe the opposite--*beating* the child spoils them for society.

It seems that most people are afraid to change their perspective on this matter. I have very few examples of family members stepping in to encourage other nonviolent methods for disciplining children. Because there's no encouragement to change, the flawed mentality continues.

So, what is the overall vision and mission of Black people in America? What should it be, and how can we turn away from these ugly actions? Collectively, where are we heading?

We have had leaders who attempted to organize and set agendas to direct the masses of Black people on a more positive course. But not since Dr. Martin Luther King, Jr., Marcus Garvey, and Malcolm X have we had leaders who were able to move the masses.

The absence of leadership could be for several reasons. Coincidently, both Dr. King and Malcolm X were murdered for the entire world to witness, and Marcus Garvey was discredited and shamed publicly before being exiled from the United States. Perhaps this prohibits other leaders from stepping up to organize and orchestrate such agendas. But part of any such plan should include ways to grow out of the slave mentality. I acknowledge that setting such an agenda is one thing--but getting a collective body to act on those plans is very difficult and requires real leadership.

The abuse I endured from my mother is now a catalyst for a much-needed, broader conversation. It is a means to inquire about what needs to happen to create positive change.

Great efforts were made to abolish slavery in the United States, and laws were passed to ensure that every state abided by them. On what is now referred to as Juneteenth (June 19th), the abolishment of slavery was complete when the last African enslaved people were freed in the state of Texas.

However, that residual evil has lingered and was further sanctioned through the use of Jim Crow laws and other blatant and systematic discrimination tactics. Although we continue to see improvement in how other ethnicities treat blacks, we are still a universe away from complete solidarity in our society.

There must be discussion centered around how to change and remove the slave mentality from ourselves as a collective. Otherwise, there will be thousands more mentally, emotionally, and physically abused young Black children who will further perpetuate this problem.

The first thing to do is create a functioning definition of what slave mentality is that can be used as a reference point when having such conversations, but this is easier said than done because the topic itself is volatile and extremely debatable. However, we must identify the baseline from which to begin the dialogue.

Once a baseline definition is established, the behavior should be openly identified as divisive because the acknowledgment of the problem creates the opportunity to find a solution.

Then, problem-solving can begin through the use of better education, access to mental health counseling, and other tools that can improve our overall mental conditioning. A holistic approach is necessary to achieve such an idea.

To truly break the chains of dysfunction, abuse, and poverty, new positive mentalities must emerge for us collectively the way they did for me. Breaking the chains and adopting such approaches can create a cultural shift on a massive scale. Are we, as a culture, at a point in our history where we are saying enough is enough? Do we have a collective desire to escape mass abuse? Are we at a point where we can identify areas that are problematic and prohibit our collective vision? Can we understand why these areas are problematic?

There are countless examples of the horrific lifestyles many African Americans lead. To help change our collective condition, I must continue to share how I escaped the jaws of abuse and reach as many people as I can with my story. It's my way of affecting cultural change.

Control Your

PART-SIX

Positively Absolutely

Over time, I learned to be a positive and faithful person. So, despite the circumstances I have endured in life, my cup is always half full--never half empty, and I immediately separate myself from those who drink from the half-empty cup. This concept is most valuable and has allowed me to remain positive in situations that would be a nightmare to others.

I had to accept that what might be considered "bad things" will happen in everyone's life; it is inevitable. We have no control over that; but since that's an inevitability, your time is better spent figuring out how to move back into good spirits by seeking out better conditions and returning to mental balance.

Presence, Sir!

So many things are competing for our attention all day: social media feeds, t.v., radio, friends, family, and work. So you must learn to be present in life as a crucial means of survival. It's hard to find your true spiritual presence if your day is cluttered with other people's thoughts, ideas, and problems. The world, and the marketing that is targeting us daily, is designed to keep our attention on products, entertainment, fear and every other agenda except our own. So, it is difficult to be positive when thoughts of fear and the lack of necessities are consistently bombarding you with negative energy. So, unplug from those things as often as you can, and pay attention to your mind, body, and spirit as often as possible.

Whatcha Thinking? Is it Important?

I work very hard to control my thinking and how that impacts my day to day activities. Thinking about solutions is very important for the avoidance of future problems. Allowing the mind to ruminate on unpleasant memories and events from your past will lead to depression. Going back in time to change the outcome of those events is impossible, and the depression it will cause won't allow you to generate positive energy, so it's best only to revisit the past as a reference point.

Thinking of the future too much is equally unhealthy. The mind can latch onto a future event and create an unlimited number of scenarios about how it might end, what could go wrong, or fantasize about ideal situations; this creates a pool of quicksand that sinks the person further down into an abyss of fear and anxiety. Once a person becomes overtaken by fear and anxiety, insanity is soon to follow. Instead, allow yourself to make quick mental notes about the future event.

The Vision that Drives Me

What could I possibly do to change the impact of all the hate I'd already experienced?

That was the million-dollar question I asked myself, which told me I had a deep desire to change my circumstances. As the old Georgian saying goes, "you can not change anyone who doesn't want to be changed." So, what could be done for someone who wanted desperately to change everything? I wanted everything about my life to be different. Pondering over the dysfunctional life I had endured terrified me, and I was not willing to repeat it or continue living that life for anything.

Honestly, changing my condition would have been hard for me if I didn't first see the need for it to change. Lacking the desire to change would've meant my circumstances were not bad enough.

So, when an opportunity for me to make a change in my life showed itself, I grabbed it and put it in a headlock, aggressively negotiating my departure from my parents' home; I wasn't taking "no" for an answer. The desire to change was my first step toward creating the kind of life I wanted; the desire burned a hole in my psyche, and I was completely consumed with the idea of freedom. That's what it takes! The desire to change is the energy that woke me from my nightmare.

Walk Through the Change

Starting the process was harder for me because of my age. However, once I was in my twenties and I thought back on that period of my life, I recognized three clear steps I took to start the process, and I have consistently repeated those steps to improve my life for the better.

The first step was to identify the issues, but it seemed that escaping them was impossible; when I saw what happened to Tommy that night, finding the desire to change wasn't hard to come by.

The second step was to understand why these areas of my life were problematic. It isn't hard for anyone to understand why abuse, neglect, poverty, depression, and overall sadness would be a problem. Thinking deeply about specific scenarios helped me further understand how these problems would impact my future if I were to stay in that environment.

The last step I took to ensure that I would not relive my past was to create multiple solutions for my problems. Identifying solutions for life problems as dark as mine seems daunting. But, I had to learn to problem-solve quickly. I had no idea what I was doing was actually part of the problem-solving phase of change.

Daydreaming about the ways I could turn all those negative and depressive episodes around and create a better life than the one I was given led me to one solution--leaving. Then I came up with other solutions, like going to college, building a career, getting married, and having children of my own that I would teach a different way to live based on my example.

Now, I think of these solutions as the baby steps that ultimately lead me to the kind of life I wanted to live. That's why all the steps are so critical in the process of starting change.

Opportunities…Seen Any Lately?

There is a clear link between identifying solutions to my problems and then pursuing opportunities that could change my life for the better. Opportunities presented themselves all the time, but it didn't mean those opportunities would be solutions to my problems. Ideal opportunities are precious and rare, but when they present themselves, they become the underground railroad through which you can escape to a better life. But you must always be on the lookout for opportunities because they can sometimes be challenging to identify. The windows to opportunity open quickly and close even faster. Your actions must be deliberate and calculated when pursuing an opportunity.

Throughout my life, there were several opportunities that I did not take. I believe that I had spiritual tour guides helping me navigate through opportunities, and l was aware of that at a very early age. I have also come to realize that opportunities should be prioritized based on how much they would change my life.

In retrospect, only a handful of those opportunities were worth my attention. The others were not even worth the time it took to determine whether they were a good fit. So, I focused my attention on the few opportunities that seemed like they were best for my situation. After I focused my attention on the best opportunities to pursue, I created a plan of action for pursuing each of them.

When I was younger, my plans were mostly in my head and in my heart; and even though I obsessed over them, my plans never fell smoothly into place the way I'd fantasized they would. As I grew older and matured, I started to plan for opportunities more strategically. I knew I needed to put feasible plans into place, not just have them floating around in my mind, and the same will likely be true for you. Concrete plans need to be made and revisited periodically to ensure that your actions are leading to the outcome you planned.

Long-Distance Vision

Here's what I know for sure: I could not have capitalized on any of the opportunities presented to me unless I knew where I ultimately wanted to go. I would have never made changes in my life if I didn't have a clear and vivid vision of my ideal life and how different that would be from what I was presently experiencing.

Because I frequently envisioned a better life for myself, identifying opportunities that could move me one step closer to that vision was simple. I saw those opportunities as possible milestones in my life that, if leveraged correctly, they could become significant points of change that would bring me closer to my ultimate vision of life.

But remember, rarely does everything go as you envision it, and hardly ever will things go *exactly* as planned. Remember our friend, Murphy, and his law about anything that can go wrong? Well, as a child, I didn't understand Murphy's law, so I felt like life was stacked against me whenever I attempted to move towards my vision.

I took everything as a personal attack on me. As a result, my self-esteem plummeted, and I fell into depression every time life presented another obstacle for me to overcome on the way to my vision. It took a while, but eventually, I learned to stay focused on my vision while remaining flexible enough to change my course of action as needed. I began to understand that opportunities would come and go, but my vision needed to remain constant. Making this subtle shift was necessary for me to maintain my sanity, self-esteem, and overall happiness. I have kept the same vision for life since I was a kid; I just add to the overall framework of my dream regularly--treating all opportunities as the means to reach my vision. This strategy keeps me balanced and allows me to focus on the desired outcome.

Seeing My Vision Through

Once I developed my vision and identified the opportunities that would help me move closer to my desired outcome, I could not get complacent. I had to see my vision through if I expected lasting change in my life.

Just because I have a vision doesn't mean it will just happen. I had to have a deep desire to see my vision through until it became a reality. A commitment was necessary; otherwise, any small failure would have caused me to give up.

What helped me continue my push--even in the face of failures and missed opportunities, was having a great support system. I had people who were there for me when I needed help the most. Having a team of caring people to support my vision and hold me accountable is extremely important. I have surrounded myself with like-minded individuals who were just as passionate about life and determined to live it successfully. And this has always been true for me.

I have vivid memories of my high school buddies who supported me and became part of my team. Cedric, Jose, Demetrius, Matthew, and I were inseparable, and they were a very positive influence on my life. We played sports together. We chased girls together. We were together constantly, and they pushed me to realize my vision more than anyone in my life besides Aunt Janette. These four guys sincerely had my back and believed in my ability to overcome adversity.

The most notable example of us encouraging and pushing each other towards greatness happened on a summer day in 1993.

We were looking for something to do to pass the time, and it was common for us to travel to a nearby town with hopes of meeting up with some new girls we didn't already know. Our means of transportation varied, but on this day, we were in Jose's big, brown van we affectionately called "Doodoo Brown." His father was a carpenter and used the van to haul his work equipment. But it was also roomy enough to fit and haul around the girls we met on that hot, summer day.

We sat around, talking and joking with them, and later, they introduced us to some players from their football team. We hung out with them for half of the day. And it was such a great day because I was happy for once! I was with my boys, we'd made some new friends, and I even got a few phone numbers! That was one of the "never forget" moments of my life. The simplicity, comradery, and fun of that day made it perfect from my vantage point.

On the way home, we were all so excited about life after having such a good day that we started talking about the future and making plans. I believe we all were in sync with each other because we seemed to be feeling similarly in that moment. We all seemed to be on the same mission; we were all searching for happiness.

Cedric was in the passenger seat; he turned to everyone and said, "Man, did you see that girl wearing those cute little shorts? Man, I think I'm in love, dawg!"

We all laughed and simultaneously responded, "Man, you just met the damn girl. How are you already in love?"

Jose while driving, turned around in his seat to throw his words at Cedric, who was just over his shoulder. He chuckled, "He's always falling in love quick, like he never saw a girl before."

I jumped in, "Yeah, man, Brooks County has some good-looking girls!"

We all paused for about three seconds. And to demonstrate how in sync we were, we all yelled with happiness and excitement, "We gotta go back over there tomorrow!"

Demetrius was a year older than the rest of us and always seemed to be a bit more insightful. His response will always sit with me as quiet motivation. It was like an alarm clock with a subtle chime that gently nudges you awake.

"Man, we have to promise each other that if one of us makes it big, we all have to make it big." He said it with so much conviction and determination in his voice.

"Oh, hell yeah, Dawg, you know dat already!" We all responded with the same conviction and determination.

That's when I knew that I was with a group of guys who wanted the same things from life as I did. I was filled with positive energy in that moment and an even deeper desire to win than I had before. I still hold on to that feeling of belonging and Brotherhood I experienced all those Summers ago. Because that group of men poured ambition into me that day, I do not get discouraged when opportunities don't show up as planned. I realize that I must believe that the best opportunities will present themselves to me. And they do. All the time!

Sometimes, opportunities and the choices I make do not move me in the direction I expected, based on my vision. Persistence is required to keep moving forward. That day, as I rode back to my Thomasville with the fellas, I was flooded with the understanding that it is very easy to make bad choices when the people around you negatively influence your thinking. That's why I appreciate that group of guys; they always pushed me forward into the arms of life and towards my vision of how I believe that should look.

Attracting Positive Energy

I also have a long list of people who, in one way or another, have negatively added to my life. These people exist and are as much of a motivation for me as the people who poured into me positively.

I recall coming home for the summer one year when I was in college. I decided to head over to my former high school to get a work out in with Demetrius. He and Coach had a special father-son type of relationship, so Demetrius felt comfortable hanging out and snooping around the coach's office--which was connected to the weight room. As I focused on my work out, I heard a high pitch voice with irritation coming from the office area.

"Corey, hey man, come here for a minute," Demetrius shouted at me in a powerful voice.

"Hurry up, Dawg, come look at this," he added to his demand.

Slightly irritated with the interruption of my workout, I went into the office saying, "Whatchu want? Dawg, I'm trying to get a work out in before Coach Johnson brings his ass up in here!"

Demetrius said in a sorrowful voice, "Here."

In his hand was a stack of envelopes. If I had to guess, there were probably about fifty envelopes.

Confused, I asked, "Man, why you in this dude's mail, bruh?"

Demetrius could not make eye contact with me and, again with sorrow, said: "They are yours, Cuz."

I looked at the stack of envelops to confirm his statement. Every one of them had my name on it. My eyes grew bigger, and my heart sank as I realized what he was showing me. They were letters from recruiters from several colleges. Letters from major colleges, like Clemson, Duke, Florida State, Georgia, TCU, and Pittsburg, populated the stack. There were smaller colleges that also extended potential offers. By that time, I had already been in college a year, so the letters were worthless. How long had they been there? Did I make the right choice based on the best information I had at the time? These were all questions that rushed my head at the time.

By this time in my life, I had become more optimistic, level-headed, and fair-minded, so I said to Demetrius, "Oh, these must have come after I graduated."

"Nah, man, look at the postmark," he said with even more sorrow. He understood where I had come from in life and how hard I had worked to achieve the successes I was beginning to realize.

But as I looked through the stack, he was right--the letters were old. Why did he keep them? Why didn't he give them to me? You mean to tell me, I actually could have had even more options?! My heart sank further as I realized another adult had conspired against me achieving my life's vision.

Whether it was intentional or not, was not as important to me. What was important was to recognize that there will always be someone who tries to force negativity into your life.

There will always be someone who tries to derail you along the journey to your vision, so it's important to pour as much positivity as you can into yourself. By thinking and living as positively as possible, you will always attract more positivity in your life. It's physics, baby... the law of attraction! Despite countless negative experiences in my life, my positive outlook always prevails.

Chains

Ancestral Chains and the Positive Impact

My ancestors were conditioned to think negatively about their lives. They were not allowed to pursue an education, or learn to read, for that matter. Families were torn apart to ensure success was not achievable in the strange land they were forced to call home. Immeasurable odds were against them, and those experiences led them to believe they were less than human; those negative messages found their place in their collective psyches and never left.

The behaviors forced on them by their masters became chronic, and remnants of these behaviors remain in place even over a century after slavery was outlawed in America. The chains of slavery are still mentally and emotionally strong.

I committ to breaking those chains. That was my vision. The grip of physical, mental, and emotional abuse had to be loosened. The poverty and dysfunction all had to be severed from my spirit if I wanted to realize a better life. Before I set out to change my circumstances, no one in my family had ever attempted to break the chains. Despite feeling like the Black sheep of the family, I pressed on to forge a path that would lead me to true freedom. I would achieve my vision, or I would die trying.

The Chains Have Dropped

Dr. Martin Luther King, during his speech in Washington, made a prophetic statement about a time when Black people could yell the words, "free at last, free at last, thank God oh mighty…I am free at last." I believe I have finally come to recognize the true meaning of his words.

I have achieved freedom by working hard to get away from my horrible past. I discovered a path to a better life for my family by having a better vision and chasing success until it lead to my personal definition of freedom.

Because of my quest, my children have never experienced mental, emotional, or physical abuse. Their perspective on life is different than it would be if I had not made those choices. By pouring positive energy into my children, I have broken the chains of the past.

I talk with them about money and investments because I want to help grow their knowledge of how money works and combat the likelihood of them experiencing poverty. We eat at the dinner table as a family and talk about each other's activities. I am committed to my family and its overall health.

Of course, my life isn't perfect, but the typical issues my family faces are easy compared to what I experienced as a child. Thankfully, I can say that I have witnessed the growth and permanent change in my surroundings.

New Positive Chains

Breaking the chains of my ancestors doesn't mean they disappear from existence. They are still there, lurking like a wolf ready to pounce. So, I must create new strategies that continue to propel my family and me into a better life. I must create a new perspective on life for my children and condition them to always move in a positive direction.

I love the saying, "I can show you better than I can tell you." It's used widely in rural Georgia, and I embrace the concept. I prefer to "do" the things that will help me realize my vision. My children will learn more in life from what I do than from what I say to them. Knowing this concept, I choose to "show them" as often as possible.

I am committed to setting the bar as high as I can to show my children that anything is possible.

Setting achievable goals and an attainable vision for their children's lives are very important things parents should do to insist on growing the Life Wealth of the family. Consistent discussions about the mental and emotional process is also an important part of building a positive family culture.

Ultimately, I am optimistic my children will gravitate to my vision about life and adopt positive life choices. My hope is that they will also lead by example when they build their families. They must be able to teach their children the same lessons that will be impactful on future generations. It's the only way to keep the torturous chains of our past on the ground where they belong, and not around our necks. I have a new vision for our lives, and there is no room for any outcome except the one I want!

One Family Isn't Enough

As happy as I should be with breaking the chains for my family, there are still countless families who have not realized they are still in chains. My family isn't the only decedents of slaves who can attest to the cruelty and dysfunction that has plagued us for centuries.

For centuries, negative mental conditioning has plagued most Black families in America, so I cannot be satisfied by seeing my family break through the blockades. This new positive mentality must spread like funny mems on Instagram. Otherwise, the battle is lost due to the sheer number of people who will continue to suffer from old ways of thinking.

The most significant obstacle for African Americans is poor mental health. We run from addressing our mental health issues, preferring to keep those problems in the back of our minds. We never open that door and clear out the harmful trash; we just recycle the negative energy from all the trauma we endured, passing the outdated behavior down like a stained shirt we've outgrown and should've thrown away instead we give it to our brother.

New positive mentalities must begin to emerge for us as a people. Breaking those chains and adopting better approaches to life can create cultural change on a massive scale.

Are we, as a people, at a point in our lives where we are saying enough is enough?

Do we have a collective desire to escape mass abuse?

Are we at a point where we are now identifying areas of our lives that are problematic and that prohibit our collective vision?

Can we understand what the problems are and make a plan to address and eliminate them?

Are we even close to finding solutions that will help us identify opportunities to realize our collective vision?

There are countless examples of the horrible lifestyles many African Americans lead. To help change our collective condition, I must continue to share how I escaped the jaws of abuse and reach as many people as I can with my message. It's my way of encouraging positivity, just as my four buddies did for me twenty-five years ago. This is another way to create cultural change, but it is not the only way. This is my vision!

Return of the Pheonix

Everyone in the world have experienced something traumatic in their lives. Whether it be the death of a loved one or physical abuse, there are experiences that cause sadness and depression in people everyday. I can not believe I am unique because of my history. There are millions of people with similar stories. There will be millions more that will go through similar or more daunting situations in the future. Bad circumstances and conditions will not end tomorrow. Instead of focusing on how horrible my past is, I prefer to bring my attention to the growth I experienced after those atrocities.

To overcome the remnant emotions of child abuse, I had to recognize that I didn't walk that journey alone. Whatever deity you chooses to believe in, is irrelevant. The choice to believe in a higher power is the greater message. I firmly believe overcoming poverty, neglect, and abuse to realize success was a blessing from that higher power. It was my responsibility to honor that bessing with my willingness to fight and attain prosperity.

My prosperity was directly proportionate to my willingness to believe in a better life. The more strongly I choose to believe, the more I acted in a manner that allowed me to experience prosperity. I believed fueled my passion to create better environments for my family and friends. Change started to happen around me. My environment, my perspective on life, my thoughts aligned with prosperity.

I changed my old rusted life into a glimmering jewel. I was practicing the old art of alchemy by taking a broken life and changing it into a prosperous one. It's the secret.

I took the experiences of my family and learned how to live better. I push for education, and less abusive ways of discipline. I put care and love at the forefront of my relationships. Eventhough I was thrown into the fires of abuse, I rose from the ashes to become a successful man. This is the essence of the Phoenix. I aspire to continue to soar through life and set a path to success for those who follow.

CHANGE

Barba, Robert, "21 Most Successful Black Entrepreneurs Throughout History," Tech.co, February 25, 2015, https://tech.co/news/21-successful-black-entrepreneurs-throughout-history-2015-02

Johnson, John H., "21 Most Successful Black Entrepreneurs Throughout History, " Tech.co, February 25, 2015, https://tech.co/news/21-successful-black-entrepreneurs-throughout-history-2015-02

https://www.census.gov/data/tables/2018/demo/race/ppl-ba18.html

About the Author

Corey Clark is an accomplished senior manager in the automotive industry for a top 20 company. Despite enduring abuse and neglect as a child, he has had many noteworthy accomplishments. Some of his accolades include college scholarships, businessman of the year, an MBA as well as being appointed on committees for several local government initiatives.

Parallel to the many accomplishments he has earned, Clark also has continued his commitment to support students who are going through similar situations he experienced. He continues to work in the community by implementing mentor programs.

He and his beautiful wife have three children, and they live in McKinney Texas.